The Muvver Tongue

The Muvver Tongue

Robert Barltrop & Jim Wolveridge

The Journeyman Press
London & West Nyack

First published by the Journeyman Press, 1980
97 Ferme Park Road, Crouch End, London N8 9SA and
17 Old Mill Road, West Nyack, NY 10994

British Library Cataloguing in Publication Data

Barltrop, Robert
  The Muvver Tongue.
  1. English language - Slang
  2. English language - Dialects - England - London
  I. Title   II. Wolveridge, Jim
  427'.1   PE3729.G7

  ISBN 0-904526-63-1
  ISBN 0-904526-46-1 Pbk

The drawing on the cover appeared in *The Sketch* of
21 May 1902 in a series entitled 'Shakespeare Illustrated
by Phil May', with the caption: 'You cram these words
into my ears against the stomach of my sense.'
(*The Tempest*, Act II, Scene 1)

*Photoset by Dessett Graphics and
printed by Interlink Longraph, London*

Contents

Foreword   1

1. Get Out of It! *Social class the key to Cockney and to misrepresentations of it. Polite address*   5

2. Made of Money *Slang about cash, clothes and food* 16

3. A Real Right Bull and a Cow *Rhyming slang as it is and is
   not. Yiddish, soldiers' and fairground terms* 28

4. Pure Vulgarity — *a product of living conditions. Swearing
   and jokes* 39

5. Social Questions *Politics, race, crime and drink* 50

6. Sally Broke the Jampot *Verbal fun of adults and children* . . . 62

7. Personal Matters *Emotional life, friendship and health;
   the relations of the sexes* 73

8. Moods and Circumstances *Phrases for all occasions:
   shopping, work, and giving vent to feelings* 88

9. Talking Proper *Pronunciation and usages. Sound and
   gesture* 99

10. Make Yourself at Home *Passing on Cockney in the family.
    Etiquette. Confrontations* 113

11. The Future of the Language *Influences of social changes
    and the media. Grounds for hope; some protests overdue* 126

Jim Wolveridge wishes to dedicate his share in writing this book to Peggy, for her encouragement; his friends Denise and Dolly, Rory and Kevin; and many other fellow East Enders for their interest and support.

Foreword

This book was conceived one Saturday morning in a cafe in Mile End Road. After the publication of Jim's pamphlet on Cockney slang, 'He Don't Know A from a Bull's Foot', he wanted to go into the subject more fully. As East Enders both, it was our mutual interest. We ordered two more coffees, and the idea did not take long to come. Outside the cafe, crowds drifted and bustled round the stalls: yobs and girls in jeans, shoppers from Whitechapel and Stepney Green and Shadwell, rabbis, women in saris. The Cockney tongue is the voice of them all.

We did not contemplate a scholarly work. Our concern is with the language used in streets and homes in the last forty years. Etymology explains the words, but only Cockney life explains the manner of their use — the epithets and ironies, slang which can be euphemism or sheer delight in verbal juggling, the curious self-parodying in deliberate mispronunciations and exaggerated errors of speech.

Much of it has originated in poverty: rich imagery for ruefulness of poor lives. This seems to have passed the scholars by. So has the ripe vulgarity which runs through Cockney speech, for its own sake and as an ingredient of phrases for every occasion; it springs from living conditions which must be known for it to be understood. That does not subtract from the humour — on the contrary, we have aimed to make an entertaining book because to Cockneys talk is nothing if it is not enjoyable.

We wanted to write for Cockneys as much as about them. The language is constantly shown as picturesque or comic, and almost invariably as inferior: it is taken for granted as coming from a people who do not know any better. We hope to persuade Cockneys as well as others that it is more than the equal of any other form of speech. Like all language, it has changed and must continue to do so: but the changes should be organic, not forced by a doctrine of 'good' and 'bad' ways to talk. In all its variety and complexity, the muvver tongue should be used with pride.

~ ~

What is a Cockney? 'Born within the sound of Bow Bells' is a myth long overdue to be demolished. A native of Stoke Poges could make the claim on the grounds that his hearing was specially acute. More seriously, there are a great many Lord and Lady Mucks whose proximity to Bow Bells does not give them the smallest share in Cockney culture.

Fundamentally, it means East End working class. Cockneyland starts at Aldgate and runs along Commercial Road and Whitechapel Road (both changing their names at various points) as far as the River Lea. The heart of it, though not the geographical centre, is Poplar. It includes Stepney, Limehouse, Bow, Old Ford, Whitechapel, Wapping and Bethnal Green. Up to the last generation all these areas held nobody who was *not* working-class, but in recent years some of the Thames-side districts have had inroads of 'gentrification'. It makes no difference; if Cabinet Ministers and heads of professions built barricades in Poplar High Street, they would still not be Cockneys.

Some other districts are what might be called 'fringe Cockney'. Hackney and Hoxton, for example, though Hackney has always had and still retains a prohibitive element of being 'select'. The Elephant and Castle area is generally looked on as Cockney, but in fact South of the Thames is a separate culture. Canning Town and West Ham have a better claim because they represent the pushing-out of the East End by industrialists who escaped restrictions by crossing the Lea. People who have moved along the railway lines to Leyton and Walthamstow have themselves repudiated Cockneydom and are anxious (or their parents and grandparents were) to dissociate from the East End.

And this brings us to the other Cockney element. As well as being a locality, it is an attitude of mind. The Cockney feels an affinity with his kind. It is hard to say he loves them (he would deny it strongly) or his surroundings (who *would* love Vallance Road or Cable Street?). Nevertheless, he is conscious that if he parted from them he would be poverty-stricken in another, less remediable way. He may be a Labourite — the majority of Cockneys are — or a more explosive radical talking about a classless society; but while this one is here he recognizes that he belongs to the working class, and is not going to pretend otherwise.

The vehicle of Cockney culture is everyday speech. That is what this book is about. When we said we were writing it, some people spoke about 'the amount of research' they supposed we were engaged in. We have done little or none; the material is what we have absorbed all our lives, and if that were not the case we should have neither the desire nor the capacity to write it. Our method of working was for each of us to write what he knew and thought under various headings, then to put the results together. This accounts for a certain amount of re-tracing, and for something else. It was impossible not to cite persons and happenings in our own lives; the reader is left to sort out which 'I' and whose old man and friends are the subjects of all these references.

~ ~

There are a lot of books depicting Cockneys and their talk and attitudes atrociously, but some which are worth reading. William Matthews's *Cockney Past and Present* is the standard book on the history of Cockney speech, and Eric Partridge's *Dictionary of Slang and Unconventional English* is a useful reference work. Julian Franklyn's *The Cockney* describes Cockney life and language with a mixture of accuracy and romanticism. For those interested in the background, what has made Cockneys what they are, Millicent Rose's *The East End of London* is an excellent study; and it is supplemented by Chaim Bermant's *Point of Arrival*, the history of immigration into East London. Michael Young and Peter Willmott's *Family and Kinship in East London* is a sociological study, but a highly readable one, of family relationships. Among personal accounts, Dolly Scannell's *Mother Knew Best* describes an upbringing in Poplar before the war and is a delight to read. A. S. Jesper's *A Hoxton Childhood* goes back farther and is grimmer but equally to-the-life.

To idealize the Cockney is only another way of parodying him. The growth of centres which seek to keep East End culture and community alive, and foster working-class writers, is undoubtedly a good thing; but the pitfall has to be avoided. Too much of what was intended as working-class literature and theatre has ended up providing chic entertainment for other sections of society (which the poets, playwrights etc. have then joined). The Cockney is a product of history. Certainly he needs voices in literature and the other arts. Our point is that you cannot develop a culture and call forth its voices by organizing to do so; they grow out of a way of life.

CHAPTER 1

Get Out of It!

Cockney speech has suffered attacks from two sides. First, educationalists have done their best to stamp it out and effect a mass conversion to 'standard English'. Second, literature and popular entertainment have created a burlesque which has heavily devalued Cockney speech and obstructed understanding of what it is about.

The academic hostility to Cockney is caused, paradoxically, by its uniqueness. It is alone among dialects and accents in being exclusively working-class. There is no other local speech which the teacher can regard apart. In the north, the west, midlands and East Anglian countryside, or if he be Scots or Liverpudlian, to a greater or lesser degree he talks the same; the accents and speech-habits are classless.

Given this, all kinds of condemnations are made. Cockney is said to be an ugly mode of speech, but when the alleged ugliness is examined it comes back to class. Thorstein Veblen observed in *The Theory of the Leisure Class* that when people find a silver spoon is only cheap metal after all, their feeling for its beauty vanishes and they discover that they think it horrid. It has been claimed that 'the best English' is spoken in Yorkshire, or alternatively by educated Dubliners; the brogues of Somerset and Scotland are considered charming. Yet each of them has characteristics parallel with those of Cockney.

In the East End, for example, they say 'aht' and 'abaht'. A better rendering of this would be 'uht', in fact; but why is it disgraceful while the Scotsman's 'oot' and the rural 'eowt' are accepted? If it comes to that, how should the 'ou' sound be pronounced anyway? Another characteristic for which the Cockney is damned is the glottal stop — reducing 't' to a grunt in the back of the throat. 'Get out of it', said thus, cannot be written down and has to be heard. There may be a valid argument that it is wrong; but the argument should not be confined to Cockney, as anyone who has heard a Scot say 'Get out of it' knows.

'Gorn' and 'orf' are more misdemeanours of Cockney speech; how surprising, then, to find that upper-class people pronounce 'gone' and 'off' like that. However, something which should be understood is that Cockneys often used — and no doubt still use — mispronunciations and grammatical atrocities as their own in-group humour. My father would say 'I'm arstin' of you', or 'it don't matter, do it?' This was not normal speech but a verbal amusement. Of course it existed because people were known to talk like that; but had they not been a nearly-extinct minority this kind of humour would have been impossible. It is important to realize the part it has played in Cockney talk. As children we said to one another 'Gissit 'ere', meaning 'Give that to me'; but at a quite early stage we became aware that a sort of mocking joke was involved.

Cockneys drop h's. So do the French, and for an English person to say ''otel', ''aricot beans' and ''ospital' is high-class, implying that he or she is a practised linguist. The teacher's case is that 'h' should be sounded on English words because this is the established practice. So it is — but not among Cockneys. They know that h's are there and put them in in writing; but to use them in speech is 'talking posh'. Their omission does not lead to misunderstandings, except by non-Cockneys. In my boyhood there was a road near the school called Helena Road, and a new boy gave his address as what sounded like ''Elena Road'. 'Spell it!' snapped the headmaster; the boy said 'E-l-e-a-n-o-r', because that was the name of the road where he lived. The teacher was ignorant, not the boy; it was a matter of *our* received pronunciation.

There is a belief that, as well as dropping h's, Cockneys add them in the wrong places and say things like: 'This hevening Hi'll 'ang these harticles hup in the 'ouse.' In our experience it is completely untrue; it has never been an idiom and is too unwieldy to be used as a joke. The Cockney was and is neither more nor less literate than the rest of the working class, and if this were an error due to ignorance it would hardly be special to East London.

The effect of a hundred years' war on Cockney speech in East End schools has been to make Cockneys accept that they talk badly. It may look as if they have persisted in doing so nevertheless; but it is not as simple as that. Some changes have been produced in Cockney speech. For example, the glottal stop has largely given way to a vague 'd' sound which turns t-less 'Get out of it' into something like 'Gedd-oud of it', as a half-hearted gesture to oblige the teachers. More than anything, however, East End children of the past forty years have tended to be bi-lingual: a speech for teachers and special occasions, another for street and friends and indoors (permutations are possible, according to circumstances). One or the other becomes dominant eventually. If the child 'gets on' at school and heads for a higher station in life than his parents', he will make the school lingo his own; if not, his proficiency at it fades through disuse after leaving school.

A defence of the way Cockneys talk could do as much damage as any attack. Like other dialects it is there, that's all; and if this is recognized, hostilities can and should cease. At twelve years old one of us was subjected, as innumerable Cockneys have been, to the gibes of a schoolmaster with a special down on East End vowels. He might have said 'My speech is as good as yours', because it was true; and had that been possible, he hopes he would have said 'yourn'.

~ ~

The growth of periodicals and light reading matter in the middle of the 19th century is usually attributed to the railways. This was before the age of workmen's trains; the readers were middle-class families wanting to have tedium relieved and be amused on journeys as well as in their homes. Given that public, the working class was an easy source of humour: servant-girls, boozers, and above all the Cockney whose life and utterances made chortles everlasting.

Dickens had a lot to do with it. George Orwell pointed out that Dickens never penned a decent picture of a working man or woman; his famous characters were drunkards, scroungers and menials. The most celebrated of all, Sam Weller, was something like a feudal retainer; yet he provided the ideas of a Cockney and his talk that lesser writers than Dickens have repeated practically ever since.

Certainly there is some marvellous humour in Sam Weller and his father. But where did Dickens get the Wellers' style of speech? Its strongest single characteristic is the exchange of v for w, as in 'Bevare of vidders', 'A double glass o' the inwariable', and such sentences as: 'I've told her how I'm sitivated; she's ready to vait till I'm ready and I believe she vill.' There is very little evidence that Cockneys ever spoke like this. Mayhew puts the v-w transposition into some of his characters' mouths, but they were costermongers in the Cut area of South London. In the 20th century the use of v for w became a feature of Jewish jokes, and the readiness of Cockneys to laugh at it suggests that they were unconscious of having used it themselves.

Nevertheless, it recurs in the 'werry good' of comic-book Cockneys, and jokes like the *Punch* cartoon of a Cockney handing his pint pot to his wife and saying: 'Drink deep, Maria. Drink werry nigh 'arf.' Sam Weller's 'young 'ooman' likewise became a stock phrase. What we have is a kind of pantomime Cockney, about as real as the Frenchman with a little pointed beard and the German who says 'Donner und blitzen!' in every other sentence. It was still going strong at the turn of the century — but a visitor who stayed in the East End in 1902 found nothing resembling it. Jack London's *The People of the Abyss* contains a lot of recorded conversation which is much more like Cockney as we know it, without Weller-*Punch*-isms.

Herman Melville also came to England and mixed with Cockneys as a seaman. His second novel, *Omoo*, contains a scene in which a landlubber named Rope Yarn is teased for his Cockney speech and ways: if he were back in London, what would he have for breakfast?

'Well, then', said he, in a smugged tone, his eyes lighting up like two lanterns, 'well, then, I'd go to Mother Mill's that makes the great muffins: I'd go there, you know, and cock my foot on the 'ob and call for a noggin o' somethink to begin with.'

'And what then, Ropey?'

'What then, Flashy', continued the poor victim, unconsciously warming up to his theme; 'why then, I'd draw my chair up and call for Betty, the gal wot tends to the customers. Betty, my dear, says I, you looks charmin' this mornin'; give me a nice rasher of bacon and h'eggs, Betty, my love; and I wants a pint of h'ale, and three nice hot muffins and butter — and a slice of Cheshire; and Betty, I wants — '

In his biography of Melville, Lewis Mumford says of this passage and the rest of the dialogue: 'Here, from an American writer, is perhaps the first clue to the existence of modern Cockney.' Melville was at sea from 1839 to 1844, and *Omoo* was published in 1847 — not many years after *Pickwick Papers*, and fewer still after *Oliver Twist*. Moreover, his rendering of Cockney is little different from Jack London's fifty-five years later. These two Americans, recording what they heard (London's book was written on the spot, day by day during his stay in the East End), give us speech which not only is recognizable today but shows Dickens's and the others' to be a fantastic misrepresentation.

Mayhew's *London Labour & The London Poor* is not evidence at all on this matter. The statements made to him by street-sellers, ragmen, scavengers and criminals are obviously reconstructed in a stagey standard English. The Wellerisms appear only when he is describing cries and quarrels, and it is clear that Mayhew's versions of speech are not faithful reportage but practical journalism. In fact he was a middle-class comic writer, joint-editor of *Punch* and the author of several comedies and farces, for one of which he wrote the Cockney song 'Villikins and his Dinah'. It looks as if Mayhew in his documentary work simply used the literary conventions for rendering Cockney speech that served for his plays and had been so firmly and profitably laid down by Dickens.

Between the two world wars 'Cockney' humour appeared in stories like the Mrs 'Arris and Bindle series. Neither character was an East Ender, but each conveyed an idea of a 'typical' Cockney. The Bindle books were written by Herbert Jenkins the publisher, who marketed Mrs 'Arris and also Thomas le Breton's Mrs May stories. Their theme was the common man's waggish philosophy always bringing him out on top (the victories were assertions of prejudice in themselves, since they were over characters the reader would like to see defeated — feminists, religious and political fanatics, etc.). The Mrs 'Arris stories, by Clifford B. Poultney, plastered together every libel on Cockneys ever devised. Mrs 'Arris, a widowed charwoman, was shown as a boozer ('there's the cork out of the fust meal as 'Arris ever tre't me to'), a sponger ('My motter is, was, and always 'as bin: If you don't see wot you want — *ask* for it!'), bone-idle and mealy-mouthed. She exchanged h's indefatigably between where they belonged and where they didn't, and piled up grammatical errors and malapropisms no Cockney would have thought of ('a large butcher 'oo's as rich as Creases'). And each of these traits was treated as *ipso facto* uproariously funny.

However, while this pernicious drivel amused lending-library readers, the music hall was still alive. In the 'twenties and early 'thirties the Cockney was able to see comedian-singers such as Harry Champion, Florrie Forde, Wilkie Bard, Billy Bennett, Vesta Victoria, Lew Lake (with his show 'Casey's Court') who represented his culture and attitudes accurately. The real calamity came with the rise of radio, which by the mid-thirties was in most working-class homes. Cockneys found themselves listening to characters like Mabel Constanduros's 'Mrs Buggins', a comic crone half-way between Bindle and Mrs 'Arris, and Sid Walker the rag-and-bone man expounding life's (supposed) little problems.

It is no use thinking Cockneys should have seen that they were being ridiculed. If they had, there was nothing they could do about it. Also, the borders between distortion and authenticity were not always easy to see; Sid Walker was somewhere near the borderline, and the East End sisters Elsie and Doris Waters did comedy dialogues which were the genuine article. Nevertheless, the working class at large were convinced that Cockneys were a race who spoke a funny language. Comedians and scriptwriters pushed the thing for all they were worth while people began to abandon the music hall for the radio and 'the pictures'.

The cinema played only a secondary part. East Enders of the nineteen-thirties grew up on it, and certainly their talk was affected by it. But it was chiefly additions of American terms and tag-lines — 'sez you', 'get movin'' and so on; and above all the wisecrack. These did not alter the character of Cockney speech but simply expanded it. Wisecracks were streamlined back-answers, and the Cockney had always thrived on those just as he enjoyed the interplay of stock phrases.

It was during the war that British films took up what radio had started a few years earlier. The East End was made a land of heroes because of its fortitude in the Blitz, and cheery Cockney soldiers and sailors were an ideal ingredient for wartime films. With a mood for realism (as long as it was romantic) in the air, films had Cockneys uttering swear-words and rattling off what was supposed to be their typical slang. The audiences in crowded wartime cinemas applauded and laughed, and went home feeling that all this betokened a new world for the common man after the war. The Cockney was left unsure of his identity. Were his outlook and language the product of East End history and poverty — or were they designed by the media for him to wear?

~ ~

The comedian Will Hay made his name with a stage sketch of a dithering schoolmaster and his boys. A lot of the comedy was about words — 'What's your name?' 'Watt' and 'Where do you live?' 'Ware', with prolonged follow-up exchanges, became national jokes. One line which joined them was: 'Go up the apples and pears, take off your round-the-houses, and I'll bring up the Uncle Dick.' It was said that this rhyming slang was used extensively by Cockneys; indeed, they hardly ever spoke without using it.

The *Sunday Express* humorous writer, Nathaniel Gubbins, noted satirically how it was being picked up in 1932:

West-end hostesses, I am assured, have gone completely gaga over the new game of talking rhyming slang. The game has been played in the East-end for years, but then anybody who is anybody knows that Mayfair loves anything new. This sort of thing is now being overheard:

HOSTESS: Has his satin and lace (grace) gone to the rub-a-dub (club or pub), Jeames?

JEAMES: Arter 'avin' 'is Lilley and Skinner (dinner), m'lady, 'e went down the frog and toad (road). 'E said, m'lady, that 'e wanted a mouthful of pig's ear (beer).

HOSTESS: Was his satin and lace hearts of oak (broke), Jeames?

JEAMES: Yes, m'lady. I lent him an Oxford scholar (dollar).

It has been the chief feature of Cockney presentations ever since. Its existence is real enough, and is discussed in another chapter. Much of it has meanings beyond those of a verbal game, and in some cases the abbreviation of a rhyme has become a word in itself: for example 'raspberry' for a blown derisive sound was originally 'raspberry tart'. But a great deal of what is supposed to be rhyming slang is invention by scriptwriters. An outstanding instance is 'berk', which was used copiously as an epithet in 'Steptoe and Son'. The story which went round was that it was a disguised obscenity, short for the rhyming 'Berkeley Hunt'. Valid as this may be, Cockneys never used the word and it was unheard-of before the television comedy series. The same is true of the Steptoe expression 'Brahms and Liszt' for 'pissed' (i.e. drunk).

There is no reason, of course, why a phrase minted in this way should not be accepted into the language. As with words generally, it happens when there is a gap to be filled. The above expressions did not catch on because there was no need for them; nor did 'Wilkie Bards' for playing-cards, from the nineteen-fifties' TV series 'The Army Game'. One media-invented rhyming phrase that has gone into general use is 'Bristols' (short for 'Bristol Citys') for the female breasts, and that was because Cockney slang and working-class speech as a whole were surprisingly short of homely terms for this anatomical item. One or two rhyming expressions existed — 'threepennies', for 'threepenny bits', and 'Manchesters' — but were never used much.

The list of known rhyming slang expressions is lengthy, but those used in everyday speech make a much smaller number. To a large extent it was employed in the parodying manner noted earlier. Referring to my father again, he would say 'Keep your mince pies a-wobbling' (for 'keep a look-out'); or 'I could do with a laugh and a joke' (a smoke); or 'I had a smack in the eye (a pie) in that coffee-shop'. He was in an expansive mood when he spoke like that; the expressions were jocularities or showpieces.

The idea that Cockneys have made such phrases permanent substitutes for words is a serious misunderstanding. They are too contrived, long and showy. Compare them with the rhyming expressions which do get used regularly. 'Can I have one of your Jimmy Riddles?' (= 'May I use your toilet?'); 'when I was in the Kate' ('Kate Carney' = the Army); 'hark at him rabbiting on' (jabbering: 'rabbit' is short for 'rabbit and pork', talk). These are not verbal extravagances, but economical and to the point. Conciseness is the soul of Cockney phraseology. Some of the most useful slang expressions are single words which convey a whole situation. An example is 'doofer' for a remnant of cigarette, pinched out and put aside: it will *do for* later on.

In the first month of the war in 1939 I saw an illustration of how the misconception about rhyming slang spread. Soldiers stationed in a suburban school painted on the wall: 'Stores — round the Johnny Horner.' Passers-by laughed and took this as a glimpse of a picturesque way of putting everything; no doubt a number of them repeated it and said it was real Cockney. In fact it was simply a joke, and the soldiers probably never used the expression when they talked. They were conscious of the public expecting masculine swagger and humour from them, and this was one way of obliging.

~ ~

Cockneys have a strong code of politeness and of respectability generally. The word for a person who breaches it is 'ignorant', meaning unforgiveably boorish. To display ill manners or bad taste is to be 'common'. 'Rude' in Cockney usage means indecent. A specially infamous sort of behaviour, to which the word 'wicked' is applied, is making mischief by spreading spiteful stories.

The basic words which every child is taught to use are 'lady' and 'gentleman'. A lady is any adult female whom one has no reason to disrespect. The lady next door, the lady in the shop; that lady is my aunt; poor old lady, she's not well. It can be heard any time, and is used in and out of a person's hearing. During the bread strike in 1977 I was in a baker's shop when one of the middle-aged female assistants gazed at a quite young woman in the queue outside and said 'Why, that lady's pregnant! She shouldn't be standing there — I remember how I felt when I was like that', and fetched a chair. The word is used as a general form of address: 'This way, lady.'

'Woman' can be taken, and intended, as an offensive word. To say 'the woman across the road' means either (a) I know nothing about her, and she must show that she qualifies to be called a lady, or (b) what I know about her disqualifies her from being called a lady. 'Man' as against 'gentleman' has not the same latent hostility, but it is unsympathetic. The phrase 'man at the door' implies a rent- or debt-collector, Council official, school attendance officer, etc.; a gentleman at the door would be someone more appetizing.

Among people who know one another there are less formal terms, of course. Women who work together speak of one another as 'girls', regardless of age, and women refer to men collectively as 'fellows'.

Thus, at the Jubilee street parties the ladies generally, but 'us girls' of any particular group, saw to the food while the fellows swept the road and put up the tables. An elderly woman is often called an 'old girl', but from someone who does not know her this can be offensive — 'lady' is the word. However, the term 'young lady' for a fellow's fiancée or steady has fallen off. It is still used but has been replaced to a large extent by the formerly middle-class 'girl friend' (probably from magazines and television). Sam Weller's 'young woman' has never been used in this way within living memory, and would be unfriendly.

Wives and husbands do not bandy each other's first names about, outside the circle of family and friends. Women say 'my husband', and some older Cockney women did not allow even this and referred to him as 'Mr —'. 'My fellow' and 'my old man' are for use among intimates, and 'my Ron' or 'my Harry' can be heard; but it is quite possible for neighbours of many years not to know each others' forenames.

A man refers to his partner as 'the wife', in or out of her presence, and any wife worth her salt insists on the use of her title. I have been present at the following conversation in a friend's house.

Friend (to me): Sit down, and she'll make you a cup of tea.

His wife (sharply): *Who*'ll make you a cup of tea?

Friend: Sorry. The wife will.

'The missis' is a familiarity, perhaps for use among friends and workmates. Expressions like 'the old plates and dishes' and 'trouble and strife' are for use only on very jocular occasions in a crowd, when it is understood that inhibitions may be dropped and nothing said need be taken to heart.

Cockneys' greetings are enquiries about one's wellbeing. 'How are you going?' or 'How are you doing?' or 'How's it going?'; 'How's things with you?'; 'What's new?' There is nothing unusual about this except that the Cockney expects and is interested in an answer. Great difficulty is experienced by East Enders who rise in the world because, in higher circles, the reply to 'How are you?' is to say 'How are you?' back. At those social levels the person who says how he is is unmannerly or a bore; but to Cockneys the question and answer are starting-points for conversation.

Ordinarily the answer to 'How are you going?' begins 'Not so bad' or 'Mustn't grumble'. The first is sometimes made more interesting by being expanded to 'Not so bad, considering', and the second is also used to end an account of minor misfortunes or problems: 'Still, mustn't grumble.' Another answer is 'Up and down like Tower Bridge' (into which one scholar has, quite mistakenly, read a sexual innuendo).

The classic Cockney greeting, 'wotcher', is not much more than an exclamation like 'Hi!' or 'What ho!' It can be made as two people pass in the street, or can preface a fuller greeting. The expression 'Wotcher, me old brown son, how are you?' is a museum piece. As with ear trumpets and button-boots, it is occasionally possible to find someone who has it in his repertoire; but it is for show as a curiosity, not for serious use.

The range of address-words used by Cockneys is well known: 'mate', 'guv'nor', 'chum', 'cock', 'duck', 'dear', 'love' and others. Though they can and do become habitual, as with the woman in a shop who says 'dear' to everyone, they are not at all meaningless. The Cockney likes all his exchanges with people to be based on a stated relationship, and the word has that purpose. 'Mate' (also 'my old mate'), 'brother', 'cock', 'mush' are equal-footing terms. 'Guv'nor' or 'guv', sometimes 'chief', contain a bit of deference; they are shopkeepers' and stallholders' address to their customers. A Cockney who finds he has used his word inappropriately — for instance, called a socially superior person 'mate' — is mortified.

'Duck', 'dear', 'love' and their variants, used by women, operate in the same way. No personal affection is implied — indeed, they rarely get used in talking to husbands or sweethearts, for Cockneys have a horror of demonstrativeness. Generally these words convey amiable equality, but a lot depends on how they are said; they may also carry motherliness (from an older woman), concern, or the common cause of women against men. 'Mister' or 'missis', as a form of address, are servile in a 'common' way. Small children may use them when, say, asking a stranger the time, and ragmen and hawkers do so; but to most Cockneys they are displeasing.

~ ~

A major change in the past twenty-five years has been in attitudes to swearing. Previously, boys swore profusely among themselves but knew they must not let adults or girls hear them doing so. Likewise, the use of 'bloody' and 'bugger' indoors by men was permissible in moderation as a sign of masculinity; but stronger words like 'bleeding' (pronounced 'bleedn' by Cockneys), and certainly the sexual swear-words, belonged to a special realm of use by men at work and in other narrowly-defined circumstances — certainly never in the presence of women and children. If a man forgot himself and uttered one of those words in front of his wife he was expected to apologize to her immediately.

In the late 'forties and early 'fifties my wife and I went regularly to football matches at The Orient. If anyone started 'effing and blinding', the men standing near us would turn on him severely: 'You mind your language! There's a tart over here!' (Sometimes the one word 'Language!' in a firm voice served as a warning and reproof.) Football programmes had notices asking men not to swear because of the 'lady patrons'. The general idea was that children were not supposed to know such words, and that their use in women's hearing was an insult as well as an embarrassment. In recent years there has been no chance of not hearing them continually. Effing and blinding is done unreservedly in public. Fourteen-year-old boys playing Sunday football shout the words in front of spectators who include their parents, and the adults' view seems to be that this is how the world is nowadays.

Obscenity is discussed in a later chapter, but the wholesale use of 'fucking' represents shifts in roles and manners rather than in morals. It has also produced a tendency, at least, towards impoverishment of the language. If what is traditionally the 'strongest' of all words comes into common use as expletive, adjective and all-purpose speech decoration, with its fellow terms, other words and phrases are left aside. The capacity for emphasis and colour is actually reduced. A flow of effs may have some impact, but what it conveys cannot compare with the effects of a wider Cockney vocabulary.

However, there are signs now of a change back. The surface reason is the over-use of sexual words in films and on television, but it is not simply distaste caused by a surfeit. What Cockneys seem to be perceiving — and reacting against — is that obscenity has become the small change of middle-class speech; or that it is put in the mouths of 'lower-class' characters by writers who have no feeling of its weight. If this is happening, it affirms that Cockney exists for social rather than linguistic reasons.

CHAPTER 2

Made of Money

The pronunciations were 'tuppence' for twopence, 'throopence' ('froopence') with a short 'oo' for threepence, '[h]aypny' for halfpenny; 1½d was 'three-aypence'. Up to 1939 all these were critical amounts. When a child asked his or her mother for a halfpenny to buy sweets, the likely answer was: 'Where do I get halfpennies from? Do you think I'm made of money?'

Money! The lack of it ruled lives in the East End. In the years of the Means Test there were families of five living on as little as thirty-two shillings (£1.60 today) a week. This was where the father was unemployed, of course, but an unskilled worker's wage was only two pounds ten shillings (£2.50) or less. Out of these princely incomes ten or twelve shillings would go in rent. Gas, soap, scouring powder, blacking and other household essentials had to be bought. Wool and cotton too: working-class wives made their families' clothes last as long as they could—a nicely-dressed child usually meant one with neat darns and patches as evidence of parental care and respectability.

In most homes there were instalments and debts to be paid as well. Shops ran 'clothing clubs' and 'boot clubs' (the off-licences had Christmas clubs, and toyshops offered fireworks clubs to help provide the gaiety for November 5); and the tallymen came round collecting payments for clothes bought on credit, usually a shilling or eighteenpence a week. Very often, new clothes were obtained from tallymen so that they could be pawned to solve immediate problems, thus creating more problems for the future. Older people who were up to their eyebrows in debt would say to newly-weds: 'Don't get anything on tally, you've never done paying.' Though it was a common condition, being in debt was felt to be shameful and was seldom admitted.

By the time everything was settled up, an unemployed family might not have much more than twelve shillings for food (today's equivalent would be about £7). With the father in work it was perhaps twice as much—or, more accurately, half as little. A halfpenny was a child's bus fare, or a postage stamp. It also bought a cigarette; small back-street shops split up twopenny packets of five Woodbines and sold them for a halfpenny each. Any small quantity was and is still called 'a ha'porth' of something. In terms of food this refers back to pre-1914, but in the 'thirties plenty of penn'orths were purchased.

'One of these days my ship will come in' was almost a cliché, and 'If I had a hundred pounds I could get back on my feet and open a small business' became nearly as commonplace. £100 was the magic sum before the war; its benefits could be calculated, but it was out of reach—in a Cockney adage, there were 'two chances, no chance and a dog's chance' of achieving it. This was still the case when, in the end-of-the-war election in 1945, Churchill announced that the Conservatives would arrange for every family to start buying a house with the £100 it undoubtedly had saved. The surprise reverberated through East London.

~ ~

Not surprisingly, there was a full vocabulary of slang terms for money.
Sixpence; a tanner, a sprarsey
A shilling: a bob, a deaner, an ogg. The words were the same in the plural, i.e. 'six bob', 'fifteen ogg'. 'A chip' was also used in the late 'thirties for one shilling only.
One-and-sixpence: eighteenpence, one-and-a-kick, a kibosh
Two shillings: two bob, a deuce
Two-and-sixpence: two-and-a-kick, half a dollar, a tosheroon
Five shillings: a dollar, a caser
Ten shillings: half a bar, half a quid
A pound: a quid, a nicker, a oncer; in the 'forties, a sheet
Silver money: snow

Money in general was dough or gelt. 'Mazuma' was sometimes used, more often by the film and radio comedians than the public. 'Rhino' came from an earlier period, but was heard occasionally (perhaps from children who saw it, and other bits of obsolete slang, in *The Magnet* and *The Gem*). 'Ackers' and 'lolly' came in during the 'forties. 'Coppers' has been used for wages collected when a person leaves or is sacked from a job—'You can have your cards and coppers', or 'Gimme my cards and coppers'; probably because departure without notice often means an incomplete week's wages.

Though the past tense has been used, the majority of the above terms are still in use, including those for coins. Decimal coinage seems not to have inspired pet-names. The amounts are recited drearily as 'twenty-pee', 'fifty-pee' and so on; the nicknames of the old coins are still employed, as far as they fit, when money is talked about. The only new-sounding term is 'little dabbler' for the decimal halfpenny, and that is derived from Cockney children's 'daddler' for the old farthing before the first world war.

Alongside slang for money, there was and is plenty for lack of it. A hard-up person is 'down and out', 'a bit short', 'on the rocks', 'on the ribs', 'on the floor', 'skint', 'stony', 'hearts of oak' or 'stone coals and coke'. A recent addition to this is 'a bit boracic': short for 'boracic lint' which rhymes with 'skint'. In that condition he hasn't got a halfpenny to scratch himself with — an irreverent departure from the pious 'not a penny to bless himself'; or two ha'pennies for a penny, nor a brass farthing or a penny to his name. Euphemistically, things are 'a bit humpty' with him (this phrase is also used to indicate serious ill-health). In really desperate need, he is 'down on the knucklebones of his arse'; he has only got a tanner between him and the workhouse or Tower Bridge, the jumping-off place for suicides.

A comment on the meagreness of a person's income is: 'You [he, she] won't get fat on that'. To have things on credit or instalment payments is 'the never-never', of course — most Cockneys say simply 'on the never'. However, there is also 'on the book', and in pubs 'on the slate' or 'on the nod': like 'on tick', these are straightforward descriptions of the techniques involved. Anyone who has a little money is said to be 'rolling in it' or 'lousy with it'. The upper class (bless 'em) are proverbially lousy with it and lousy without it.

~ ~

In days of mass unemployment, lack of decent clothing was the cause of bitter resentment. It was probably heightened by the proliferation of garment manufacturers in the East End. The 'poverty trap' existed when a man was shabby because he was out of work, and could not get work because he was shabby: 'how can you go looking for work dressed like a tramp? If you go after a job you have to look a bit near the mark.' When the mood was philosophical or humorous, the want was still there: 'If I only had a job, a decent suit and a couple of quid in my pocket, I wouldn't call the King my uncle.'

A child in a poor Cockney family in the 'twenties and 'thirties had ambivalent feelings about new clothing. He longed for a new suit of his own, and got one every Christmas — but only for Christmas. However hard-up the family was, the children would be expected to be smartly dressed for Christmas. So just before the festive season the tallyman came and fitted him up with a brand-new 'whistle'; but the day after Boxing Day the suit had to go to the pawn-shop, so it had to be kept spotless. Thus, his enjoyment of it was restricted. He dared not get the slightest speck on it, nor could he sit comfortably for fear of creasing the gutkas (Yiddish for trousers). It was almost a relief when Christmas ended and the suit went to Uncle's.

These experiences and attitudes have left their mark, and it is almost a ritual to pull the leg of anyone who appears in new clothes. It stops short of derision, and in fact is a way of expressing admiration (though it may lead to critical comment). A male person 'dressed up to the nines' is almost certain to be told he looks 'like a pox-doctor's clerk' (a politer variation is 'like a bookmaker's runner'). For either sex, it is 'done up like a dog's dinner' or 'made up like a hambone', and asked what he or she is going to wear for Sundays. Someone wearing a new hat is liable to be greeted with cries of ''At done it!' and 'old Rottenhat!', and if the wearer is male and the titfer is a large one: 'If you can't fight, wear a big hat.' A too-small hat is said to look like 'a pimple on a tea-tray'.

Nevertheless, Cockney girls are expected to make the very best of their appearance. Charles Booth's researchers in the 1880s remarked on the brilliant style of the Bow match-girls when work was over. In the past it was usually a short-lived bloom, a temporary defiance of poverty but soon extinguished by it. Over the past forty years, better incomes and nutrition have confirmed the brilliance. Whether in lacquered hair-dos with smart dresses, or casual gear and jeans, East London girls are astonishingly attractive by intention (immigrants quickly get the idea). It is a matter not only of sexual attraction, but of social classes' attitudes to it; the relative dowdiness of middle-class girls shows a different frame of mind altogether.

'Clobber' formerly meant old clothes, then was used for special kinds of clothing, e.g. tramps' clobber, football clobber; but since the 'twenties it has meant clothing in general. 'Gear' has a shorter but similar history — from special equipment it came to mean way-out or trendy garments in the 'sixties, and is now used for clothes at large. Clothing is also 'schmutter', but this is chiefly reserved for up-to-the-minute, dressy stuff.

Most other words for clothes are rhyming slang for various items.

Suit: a whistle, or whistle and flute

Hat: a titfer, or tit-for-tat

Trousers: round the houses

Collar: a holler boys holler

Shirt: a dicky dirt (this was never abbreviated to dickey — a dickey
was the stiff front worn with evening dress
Gloves: turtles, or turtle doves
Boots: daisies, or daisy roots
Socks: almonds, or almond rocks; less often, Chatham (or Tilbury)
Docks
Pocket: sky, or sky rocket

All of these terms are still in use, though several of them were given in
the first list of rhyming slang, published in 1837. Two expressions
which, mercifully, have practically vanished now are 'cut-downs' and
'reach-me-downs'. The first was for a father's or older brother's old
trousers with the legs cut off to make short trousers for a young
schoolboy; it was quite common, and was a conspicuous sign of poverty
because of the excess material in the waist and seat. 'Reach-me-downs'
means ill-fitting second-hand clothing for either sex; it combines the
idea of garments being handed down with that of amateur tailoring to
make them longer. Another disappearing expression is 'potato' or
'spud' for a large hole in a sock. Its origin may have been in the practice,
which was quite widespread among elderly men and women in the past,
of going about with a potato bulging in the sock or stocking as a
supposed cure for rheumatism: the hole was made by the potato, or was
pretended to be not a hole at all but the potato showing through.

A saying for new clothes, old-fashioned but still heard sometimes, is
'I wish you well to wear it [them]'. It is thought to have been Jewish —
an outfitter's blessing as his customer leaves? — but it embodies the
idea of certain garments being lucky for the wearer. The same is said
about dwellings: 'This has been a lucky house for us.' There is an echo
of it in Shaw's *Pygmalion*, when Eliza throws Higgins's slippers at him:
'Take your slippers; and may you never have a day's luck with them!'

~ ~

Food is grub. An older term is 'manger', pronounced marnjee — the
French colloquialism for eats, brought back by soldiers from the First
World War. In recent years younger people have adopted 'nosh', and a
meal is a 'nosh-up'.

Slang terms for food are as follows:
Jack the Rippers: kippers
Spotted Dick: currant pudding
Duff: plain pudding; or plum duff, treacle duff, etc.
Frog spawn: tapioca
Doorsteps: thick slices of bread
Horn sticks: celery

Kate and Sidney: steak and kidney
Suckers: sweets
Cart grease: margarine
Bread and scrape: bread thinly spread with margarine
Spuds: potatoes
Char, Rosie Lea, you-and-me: tea
Sergeant-major's: extra-strong tea

~ ~

Oscar Wilde said the only people who think about money as much as the rich are the poor. This explains not only the plethora of Cockney expressions for money, but the fact that they are supplemented by words from upper-class speech: 'spondulicks', 'oof', 'shekels', 'the needful' and even 'financially embarrassed' (said, of course, in a mock-serious manner to deflect the remark 'swallowed a dictionary?'). Another well-known bit of irony is for one person to say with pretended piety 'Money is the root of all evil' and another to respond: 'I'll have a bit of the root, please.'

Another word for money is 'drop', but it means 'takings' and not money in general. Thus, if A collects cash in which B has an interest, B may ask: 'Did you get the drop?' — or, if A delays handing it over: 'Give us the drop.' The word has been elaborated into 'dropsy' and is often heard in that form nowadays. Properly speaking, 'drop' or 'dropsy' means a discreetly-given gratuity. It is *dropped* in the palm. There is a mime of it, arm behind back, wrist pressed to buttock, hand turned outward in readiness. To make known that an off-the-record payment will be expected in some situation, one says 'You've got to drop the bloke.' It is the recipient who is said to be dropped, not the money.

Because this is a descriptive term, it covers smallish hand-to-hand transactions only. When talking about big-time ones a person is said to be 'bunged'. The idea is exactly the same. It conveys a wad of notes being stuffed by A into B's inside pocket or his briefcase or his drawer: a quick, purposeful pushing action. When bribery in high places is in the news, Cockneys agree that it encompasses lots of politicians and business men: 'They all get bunged, don't they?'

Calling on some one to disgorge cash, the phrase is 'dub up' or 'dub out'; 'cough up' and 'fork out' are middle-class schoolboys' expressions. 'Hand over' has a certain appeal because it makes a comic-book bad joke — 'The Highwayman, by Ann Dover'. When a man counts up his money he has 'a roll call'. In the past this was not a frequent necessity. A five-pound note was a marvel to behold, and a

working man who had one was treated as a suspicious character.
Shopkeepers would have nothing to do with it (most small shops did
not have five pounds in change anyway), and he had to go to a post office
where he was required to explain himself and write his name and
address on the note.

Meanness has always been unforgiveable to Cockneys, and there are
a number of eloquent phrases for it. The word used by children is
'mingy', carrying a contempt which is more or less absent from 'stingy'.
'Tight' means ungenerous, reluctant to part; and the Cockney turns
'close' into 'near' — 'Gawd, he isn't half near'. The person notorious
for his nearness is 'tight as a gnat's arse'. As an even stronger degree of
meanness, he 'wouldn't give you the drippings of his nose' (a coarser
version is 'wouldn't give his shit to the crows'). If he is the sort who
would descend to any pettiness for his own advantage, he 'would skin a
turd for a farthing'. On the other hand, there is some grudging
admiration for the person who seems to prosper in all circumstances: 'if
he fell down the lavatory' (it used to be 'in the midden') 'he'd come up
with a gold watch'.

Cadging is 'mumping'. To try out somebody for a loan or dropsy is to
'tap' him, and to try to rouse sympathy for one's needs is to go 'on the
earhole'. These terms are used for all classes of askers, the parson
appealing for a lofty cause equally with the most disreputable
scrounger. To someone who has no money to give they look the same,
'holding their hand out'. I remember a friend's father asking a
Salvation Army collector how many Self Denial Weeks a year they had.
'Oh, only one, sir!' said the young man. 'Then you're bloody lucky',
said my friend's father. 'I have fifty-two.'

An aspect of working-class money language that is unlikely ever to
return was the use of prices as, virtually, descriptive adjectives.
Children said 'p.o.' meaning 'piss off', but if questioned they said it
stood for 'penny orange' because oranges were always a penny each.
There were penny buns, penny ices ('late nights and twopenny ices'
was an ironic term for a life of extravagance and dissipation), penny
writing books, penny packets of all kinds of household things; and in
each case the type, size and quality were defined exactly by the word
'penny' — the term 'penny whistle' is still with us, a miniature flute
made of tin. Journals like *The Wizard*, *The Hotspur*, *The Magnet* and the
rest were called 'twopenny books'. 'A threepenny and a penn'orth' was
the standard adult-size meal of fish and chips (a twopenny and a
penn'orth was a meaner portion altogether).

This use of price as a description was, and to some extent is still, echoed in East End slang. To call something 'twopenny-ha'penny' dismissed it as inadequate or of no account. 'Twopenny' had the same effect; 'I don't give a twopenny fart' meant 'I couldn't care less'. In a different context, a man might pour scorn on some object or person by saying: 'Him? Twopence!' 'A twopenny all-off' was a cheap, crudely-executed haircut ('proper' barbers charged sixpence for men and fourpence for boys, pre-1939). Higher figures indicated things to be taken more seriously. When a mother said she would land her offspring 'a fourpenny one' for misbehaviour she was threatening a full-weight, first class clout — 'round the earhole', of course.

~ ~

Money provided a lot of Cockney vocabulary because it was the main preoccupation. There was never a comparable amount of slang for clothes; they did not figure prominently in a hard-up world. Indeed, references to them often appear in phrases about poverty. 'The arse out of one's trousers' is the symbolic expression for being on the rocks — in the past, if there really was a hole in the seat of the trousers (it was a not-uncommon sight) somebody was bound to say 'I see you've been arsed out'. Boots or shoes came in several graphic phrases for destitution, because of the discomforts when they were worn out and because they were an expensive item. 'Down on one's uppers' summarizes the position; likewise, 'my boots are half off my feet'. 'My boots are nearly worn down to the laces' is more jocular but just as desperate. In 1948, when my wife was pregnant with our first child, she remarked to a Cockney friend that she would be glad when it was all over. 'You won't say that when you've had half a dozen', said the old woman. 'You'll say: You stay there as long as you can, mate — while you're in there I haven't got to buy shoes for you.'

Slang about clothes was further restricted by the fact that under-garments were not talked about. Men, women and children all wore vests with sleeves; without them you would 'catch your death of cold', but nobody discussed them or joked about them. The same applied to the corsets which older women wore. Words like 'knickers' and 'panties' were unknown — that garment was called 'drawers' or 'bloomers', and both words were considered 'rude'. However, girls and young men did nickname the type which had legs with strong elastic in them 'passion crushers', and the term spread through the women's services during the war.

Most men slept in their underwear, and in cold weather their shirts and socks too. But to have reasonably clean underthings was essential to respectability. Mothers said to their children: 'If you had an accident and were taken to hospital, think how ashamed I'd be!' There was a reason why children tried to avoid changing their underwear: newly-washed cheap woollen vests were unbearably tight and scratchy. Among men's clothes, 'coat' meant 'jacket' (hence the quip: 'Do you want to fight? I'll hold your coat for you'), and the waistcoat — worn as pullovers are now — was called 'weskit' or 'weskut'.

But food was of paramount importance. The Cockney philosophy has always been that the little one gets should go first and foremost to filling bellies. It was reflected in music-hall songs like 'Boiled Beef and Carrots' and 'Food, Beautiful Food', and in 'Oh, me taters and me hot fried fish' (which goes to the tune of 'By Killarney's Lakes and Dells'); and in a parody of a musical-comedy song called 'Navaho':

> Starve her, starve her, starve her, Joe —
> If she has a bloater, pinch the roe-oh-oh-oh!
> You bet your mother-in-law will go
> If you only starve her, Joe.

The Cockney expresses his contempt for suburban values in the phrase 'lace curtains and kippers'; it means keeping up appearances at the expense of food, a way of life he regards as detestable. The same estimation is in the saying 'He's had more jobs' (or other comparisons such as 'she's had more men') 'than I've had hot dinners'. Wage-labour used sometimes to be described as 'earning a crust of bread', but this was an excessively humble view and the phrase now has a sarcastic application — 'Earning a crust, then?' as a greeting to someone known to be in the money.

Satisfying food is often said to 'eat nicely', and greengrocers chalk 'good eaters' on the price-tickets of their apples and plums. (Before anyone laughs, the grammatical switch is the same as in 'looks nice', which is said by everyone.) The only word for a truly filling meal is 'blow-out'. 'Bellyfull' means a surfeit in the unpleasant sense, as in 'I've had a bellyfull of that noise'; and 'skinfull' is reserved for drink.

To the list of slang words for food 'gippo' must be added. It is said to be a variation of 'jipper', a dialect word for meat juice which is in the Oxford Dictionary. Basically it means gravy, but it is used for any sauce or runny part of food. It is further extended to cover any kind of organic messiness: 'My boil burst last night, and you should have seen all the gippo.' Bread is used to make poultices, and this leads to the pleasantry 'Got something wrong with your hand?' when a person is seen holding an extra-large slice of bread or hunk of bread pudding.

Eating-houses or **tea-shops** are called 'coffee shops' by older

Cockneys. In the late nineteen-thirties they began to style themselves 'cafes' and consequently to be called 'caffs'. The advance in pronunciation, sounding the e, is due to hearing Nescafe persistently advertized on television since the 'fifties. The origin of 'coffee shop' lies a long way back, presumably in the 19th-century coffee-houses. Up to 1939 coffee was a middle-class drink; coffee shops sold tea, and if anyone asked for a cup of coffee there was a sense of upheaval and much byplay with a rarely-used bottle of Camp.

A well-known lady novelist in the 'thirties wrote: 'Mrs Catchpole poured the tea, which was as strong as Mary had feared it would be.' Cockneys have no use for weak tea. A good cup of tea is brim-high in a good-sized cup, rich brown and very hot. If it is not poured to the brim the recipient may say witheringly: 'Evaporates quick, doesn't it?' and if it is less than scalding he denounces it as 'cold' (one phrase for a cup of tea is 'a nice cup of hot'). Pale-coloured tea is 'gnat's', which is short for 'gnat's piss' (if bad-tasting, it is 'cat's' on the same principle). Another condemnatory statement is 'It isn't weak, it's helpless'. People who move out of the East End often start saying that they do not care for strong tea, as a sign that they have risen in the world; Cockneys in turn allege that weak tea is all suburbanites can afford.

Greediness is deplored by Cockneys. The basic reason may be economic, that a voracious person deprives the rest of his household; but there is also a dislike for that kind of behaviour — it is on a par with the Cockney's distaste for showing his emotions. Anyone who is immoderate over food is a pig, or a greedy pig. He (or she) is called 'greedy guts' or a 'greedy-gutted sod'; if the accuser is good-humoured about it, the epithet is just 'guts'. The sort of person who would eat you out of house and home is said to eat like a horse: e.g. 'She stayed last Christmas and ate like a bloody horse'. Another term occasionally used is 'gormandizer'. It conveys not gluttony but being more than fond of one's belly — which is a fair summary of *gourmandise*.

Cockneys eat dinner in the middle of the day. On any occasion when it is postponed, they feel that dinner at teatime or in the evening is abnormal and will say 'We're keeping quality hours today'. 'Lunch' is a snack taken to work or school for the middle of the morning. The final part of dinner is nearly always called 'afters'; in cafes it is called the 'sweet', and this is used in some homes as a superior touch. The word 'afters' sometimes produces 'befores' for the main course.

Ketchup and bottled sauce are used liberally in East London. They are taken for granted now, but in the past they were an attempt to give flavour to uninteresting food. An old wisecrack was 'I'm having a hot

dinner — bread and cheese and mustard pickle'. The common phrase
for being famished is 'starving hungry'; in recent years 'my belly thinks
my throat's cut' has come into fashion. A small helping of food is
described as 'not enough to feed a sparrow', and it is said of a person
who seems to exist on very little nourishment that he or she 'doesn't eat
enough to keep a sparrow alive'. (Note, however, that the old Cockney
saying 'starving the sparrows' was about a different matter. It referred
to the activities of the road-sweeper in the days of horse traffic — from
sparrows' habit of pecking at dung.)

There is a mistaken idea that Cockneys have a picturesque term for
every item of food, and go into cafes calling for 'a baby's head' for a
meat pudding, 'Adam and Eve on a raft' for eggs on toast, and so on.
These were made known in popular papers and boys' journals in the
'thirties as slang used in the catering trade. Whether that is true we
don't know — we are sceptical — but they were never part of the
Cockney language, and are too roundabout to be adopted by it. One
tag-line that has been worn threadbare but is still used, mostly in cafes,
is 'You're sweet enough, eh?' when someone specifies no sugar in his
tea. A young man said it when I was ordering tea at a coffee stall not
long ago. I said 'That crack is ancient', and he said: 'You should know,
mate.'

~ ~

Some food terms get into different contexts. 'Scraggy' for an under-
nourished person comes from the scrag end of lamb or mutton, a piece
which is mostly bones and is bought to make stew. 'In a stew' itself
means agitated or in difficulties. 'Mutton dressed as lamb' is said about
an older woman trying vainly (in both senses of the word) for a youthful
appearance. 'Mutton-eye' is one of the rather cruel nicknames for
someone with a squint. 'Fish-face' is less pointed, and is mostly used by
children as a mild insult; strictly, it is for a person with staring eyes.
('Eyes like cod's ballocks' is the more graphic adult phrase.) A few
words for food have been overtaken by ambiguity, and those using
them have to frame their sentences carefully. No-one serving chicken
or turkey in the East End today would dare to ask 'Do you want
stuffing?' and the standard answer to a waitress's 'Would you like a
roll?' is 'Yes — on the floor, with you'.

Another expression, heard in three or four different forms, is 'like
two of eels' or 'like two of drip' (i.e. like a portion of stewed eels or two
slices of bread-and-dripping). It means at a loss, not knowing what one
is supposed to do: 'left standing there like two of drip'. The picture is of
food served up and waiting on the plate for a customer who has

vanished. 'Crummy' is even more complex. It is the word for scruffy and neglected, and was used of living conditions or houses or whole neighbourhoods. It was 'crumby', of course; but the 'crumbs' were lice in the beds and furniture.

CHAPTER 3

A Real Right Bull and a Cow

Contrary to the popular belief that rhyming slang is almost the whole of the Cockney language, in the early nineteen-thirties its currency was quite small. Expressions such as 'my old pot and pan' for 'my old man', 'a bull and a cow' for a row, and 'would you Adam and Eve it?' for 'would you believe it?' were used in a casual way without any special emphasis. They were part of a range of humorous expressions of various kinds, and many Cockneys were not even aware of the term 'rhyming slang'.

I learned it when I was eleven; my father said that one of the neighbours was 'Lakes of Killarney'. I asked him what he meant. 'Off his onion. Barmy. It's rhyming slang.' He then gave a few more examples — 'Cain and Abel' for table, 'round the houses' for trousers, 'Duke of Kent' for rent, 'half-inching' for pinching, etc. I recognized the idea in other phrases I knew, and was amused but not particularly impressed; and in a short time I forgot all about it.

However, this was the period when, because of stage and radio, rhyming slang began to reach and be imitated by an audience outside the East End. Cockney comedians (real and spurious) made it an 'in' thing, and the false impression was created that has remained ever since. It occurred in Carol Reed's film *A Girl Must Live*, where Renee Houston said: 'Take a butcher's hook at this.' Cinema audiences found it hilarious; at almost the same time, just before the war, they rolled in the aisles as the first monumental 'bloody' was uttered in the film version of *Pygmalion*.

The false impression was a matter of proportion. Certainly Cockneys said 'take a butcher's' for 'look' — they still do; but not universally, or even the majority of times. At that time the commonly-used terms were 'dekko' and 'screw': 'Screw this coming up the road! What's it put you in mind of?' 'Dekko' was a gypsy word: 'Let's have a dekko.' 'Get a load of this' was also popular, from American films.

Probably it was inevitable that the amusing properties of rhyming slang would be overworked. Nevertheless, a balance might have been restored but for two things. One was the war; six years in which comic entertainment was promoted heavily, for the sake of morale, with 'the common man' at its centre. The other was a combination of scholars and journalists who found in rhyming slang a linguistic gold-mine. It was said to have been a secret language. From being a feature of Cockney talk, it turned into the essence of it. At this point questions arose but were never answered. Words and phrases may be found to exist, but the frequency of their use has to be shown as well. Thus, many terms have been resurrected that were seldom or never used. Others have simply been invented, and it is hard to draw a line; often, aptness and wit suggest that they *could* exist, and finding the reasons why they do not involves going beneath the surface of Cockney life.

An illustration may bring out some further points (it has appeared in print): 'Let's take a ball of chalk, up the frog and toad, round the Johnny Horner into the rub-a-dub, and have a pint of pig's ear.' All of these phrases are known. Only 'round the Johnny Horner' and 'pig's ear' have ever been used to any extent, and neither is specially popular. All five in one sentence is absurd; it might be a comedian's line, devised to bring a round of applause for ingenuity, but has no relationship to everyday speech. 'Let's take a ball of chalk' and 'up the frog and toad' are too long-winded and cumbersome to be realistic. Cockney is quick-flowing; its nature is to avoid circumlocution ('going all round the houses'). A much more likely version of the sentence in question is: 'Let's have a mooch up the boozer for a quick half.'

On the other hand, expressions like 'a ball of chalk' may be used one at a time for exhibitionistic purposes. This is mild fun, initiates showing off to one another with a touch of parody. They may bring out rhyming phrases — the more improbable-sounding the better — to impress an outsider; and it is possible to imagine a scholar or two being thoroughly misled by waggish Cockneys in this way.

Here is a list of some rhyming slang expressions, with notes on their use and non-rhyming alternatives.

Head: loaf or crust, short for loaf or crust of bread. Other slang words for the head are 'napper', 'noddle' and 'bonce' ('noddle' was probably a corruption of 'nodder'). 'Loaf' means the head as brain-box: 'use your loaf'. 'Noddle' is the same: 'he uses his noddle', and 'once he gets an idea in his noddle there's no shifting it'. 'Bonce' and 'napper' mean simply the physiological head: 'a bang on the bonce'. So does 'nut'; but *the* nuts are the testicles, and a [k]nut is either a comical person or a deranged one

Eyes: mince pies, almost always abbreviated to 'minces'

Feet: plates of meat, or plates

Hair: Barnet, short for Barnet Fair

Hands: Germans, short for German bands. Never widely used; 'mitts' and 'maulers' are much more common, as in 'Keep your thieving maulers off, mate' and 'Give us your mitt'. The most popular word for hands has always been 'dukes'. It is used for boxing — 'Put your dukes up', 'He can use his dukes'. The singular also is used: 'Show us your duke'. Despite a complicated explanation given by Partridge, the word probably comes from 'dukkeris', the gypsy word for hands

Mouth: north and south, always used in full — 'north' on its own would be difficult to enunciate and hear

Stomach: Darby Kell — rhyming for 'belly' with the y cut off the end of 'Darby Kelly'. This has probably survived solely on account of Harry Champion's 'Boiled beef and carrots' song:

> That's the stuff for your Darby Kell,
> Keeps you fit and makes you well.

'Bread basket' is boxing slang for stomach: 'Hit him in the bread basket' — but, because it is a euphemism, is also used as a 'polite' slangy term.

There is no rhyming slang for legs. They are 'pins': 'he's a bit weak' (or 'none too steady') 'on his pins'. Nor is there a rhyme for nose. Words used for it are 'conk', 'hooter' and 'snitch'. 'Snitch' is used mainly by children, and 'hooter' is another boxing term. A markedly red nose is called (phonetically) a rarzo, which is short for raspberry.

Sense: eighteenpence — 'haven't you got no eighteenpence?'

Cheek (in the sense of effrontery): once-a-week

The sun: currant bun

Shave: a dig in the grave

The last two expressions are used in a jocular way, as is 'taters' or 'taters in the mould' for freezing cold. Other sayings for nippy weather are 'it's cold enough for a walking stick' or 'for a suit of waistcoats' — plus, of course, the magnificent 'cold enough to freeze the balls off a brass monkey'.

The rhyming slang phrases which get used regularly are those which make points. 'Trouble and strife' and 'skin and blister' are examples; they are epigrams of how (at times) a bloke feels about his wife and sister. 'Gawd forbids' for kids is in the same vein, a reminder of the fear of having more mouths to feed. 'A bull and a cow' likewise evokes a fearful confrontation between husband and wife. 'Mutt and Jeff' (originally from a pair of silent-film comedians) is slightly cruel, though after many years' usage nobody reflects on that; it embodies a misfortune of deafness, the impression of thick-headedness that being hard of hearing often gives.

'You're a holy friar', which is a good-natured way of saying 'You're a liar', voices the idea (pretty common among Cockneys) that people in religious orders are not to be taken seriously. 'Joe Soap', for 'dope', would be a name for a simpleton even if it did not rhyme. 'Hard bake' for cake is mild mickey-taking; so is 'whistle and flute' — always abbreviated to 'whistle' — for a suit. 'Bees and honey' for money is about industriousness, and 'in a two and eight' for 'in a state' depicts an aimless muddle. 'A ding-dong' for a rip-roaring party not only rhymes with sing-song but suggests noise heard all over the neighbourhood like church bells. 'Rabbit', short for 'rabbit and pork' = talk, is kept for excessive talkers and its use in this sense is probably due to its resemblence to 'jabber': 'Hark at him rabbiting on!' or 'Can't old Charlie rabbit!'

A few of them are used as euphemisms; a rhyming phrase is a means of avoiding a blunt word. Not many Cockneys care to say 'naked' or 'nude' in mixed company, though among men the expression 'stark ballock naked' can be heard. 'In the rude' gets round it (in the past few years women and schoolchildren have taken to 'in the nuddy'). Shortenings like 'Bristols' and 'Hampton' have the same function. In the hot summer of 1976, with T-shirted girls everywhere, I heard a young man say to another 'Cor, there aren't half some Bristols about!'; I doubt if he would have said the four-letter word quite so readily. 'Orchestra stalls' for the testicles is another euphemism, though it also conveys an important place in the front.

It is not only sex that gets the edges softened by rhyming terms. 'He's done some bird' is information that a person has been in prison (bird-lime = time), and 'tea-leaf' means thief. In both cases the unpleasant-sounding forthright statement is avoided — Cockneys do not like those words to be thrown about. 'Four-by-two' is often used by people who don't wish to be heard using the other and more direct nicknames for Jews. 'Lakes of Killarney' has the same purpose. So, probably, has 'Irish jig' for a wig (humour for what might otherwise be an offensive remark on someone's appearance). In addition, there are the many rhyming terms for poverty.

~ ~

How did it originate? The theory that it was a secret language used by costermongers and criminals does not hold water. Both groups, and others which might be suggested, had and have their own slang. If there was a secret, it does not seem to have been closely kept. But the fact is that there has never been sufficient usable rhyming slang to form a language or code. It has not related to any special subject or activity, and is simply a miscellaneous collection of phrases based on words which lent themselves to the treatment. The popularization of it in the last forty years has given the impression that Cockneys have a full vocabulary of it. Nothing of the kind has ever existed.

Had that been the case, rhyming slang would not have remained uniquely Cockney. It did so, until mass entertainment discovered it, precisely because it was a minor feature of a complex language and so was little known-about. The search for a specific cause of origin for it in East London is a mistaken one. The origin is the natural tendency, wherever words exist, to make jingles and alliterative phrases (the Cockney version of this is 'You're a poet and don't know it'). According to Partridge in *Slang Today and Yesterday* (1933), it was used by a few dealers and news vendors in the provinces before 1914. Some rhyming phrases which are known today existed in rural areas in the 18th century and earlier, and must have been carried into East London in the great industrial influx. The Cockney did not invent rhyming slang but has preserved a certain body of it, when others have passed over its possibilities or dropped it.

'Authentic' slang is that which gets used. There can be arguments over this, since different groups and families may adopt terms which are scarcely if ever heard elsewhere; or they may have versions (perhaps mis-heard ones) of their own. A wide experience has to be the judge, and it is important if the Cockney language is to be distinguished from invention and caricature. The point is not to establish a canon of perfect or permitted Cockney — that would be disastrous as well as ridiculous — but to have a perspective.

There is a useful list of slang terms, rhyming and otherwise, in Ron Barnes's East London book *Coronation Cups and Jamjars*. However, it includes a few which are plainly one family's own sayings, and two outright mistakes. 'You and me' is said to mean a flea, and 'toe rag' a cigarette. Throughout the East End 'you and me' means tea — 'What about a cup of you and me?' — and is occasionally used for a visit to the lav. There is no rhyming word for fleas; they are usually called 'hoppies', from their athletic habits. A verminous person is 'cooty', and a person seen scratching him- or herself is likely to be asked 'Have you got lodgers?'

Nor has cigarette or 'fag', the universal name for one, ever had a rhyming synonym. The nearest thing is 'drag', which rhymes with fag but refers to the act of smoking a cigarette (another expression for a smoke is 'a spit and a draw'). But a 'toe rag' is decisively a person of low character, a scheisspot, a twicer, someone you wouldn't trust as far as you could throw him; it was originally a nickname for a tramp or down-and-out, and is a grislier version of the American 'bum'. Because of the value of books such as *Coronation Cups and Jamjars* in describing East End life, it must be hoped that these things will be corrected in a future edition.

~ ~

Cockney is a tongue of tongues. Any likely word or snippet from another language or jargon is incorporated and given new life in it. Many come from immigrants, whose epithets and tricks of speech have only to sound lively enough to be quickly borrowed. It works through temporary emigration too; Cockneys in groups away from home fasten on whatever term appears to fill a gap or be an improvement on what they have. Peoples who mix with East Londoners must expect to have their verbal pockets picked.

Before 1914 and 1939 economic pressures, unemployment most of all, made it fairly common for young Cockneys who were fit enough to join the Army for eight or twelve years. It gave them lodgings, food, clothing, and security of a sort; and they saw the world. In those days of the British Empire, soldiers went to the near and far east and acquired scraps of lingo; and those who had this experience were numerous enough to put words into common currency when they returned to the East End.

Thus, 'buckshee' is the Cockney word for free (in the sense of costing nothing) — strictly speaking, it means surplus or going begging and therefore available. 'Doolally' is demented, barmy. 'Let's have a shufti' or 'a quick shufti round' means a look to inspect something; the u is pronounced like oo in 'book', but in 'juldi' for 'hurry up' it is flat as in 'but'. These are straight borrowings from Hindustani. Another term which at least owes its origin to the north-west frontier of India is 'Khyber', short for Khyber Pass and rhyming slang for the backside.

'Ackers' for money came from the middle east. So did 'bint' for a girl, but this word has never caught on with Cockneys (probably because it includes 'girl' in the sense of a prostitute); it is more likely to be heard in West London saloon bars among middle-aged ex-junior-officers. 'Goolies', for the testicles, is used fairly commonly in male company only. A widely-used term which sounds exotic is 'mogadored', meaning at a loss, stumped: 'I'm mogadored', 'that had him really mogadored'. Mogador is a port on the coast of Morocco. However, the word comes from the Romany *mokardi* or *mokodo*, which has also produced 'put the mockers on' something = to jinx it. It refers to gypsy taboos: the *mokardi* article is tainted and has to be destroyed.

The two world wars have acted as linguistic melting-pots. The slang of the various services spread among civilians, and some local expressions became and have remained national ones. An outstanding example is the Lincolnshire dialect word 'skive'. Its meaning is not so much to evade duties as to perform them evasively: a situation so readily recognized by servicemen that the word was taken up everywhere and by the nineteen-fifties was part of the English language.

Cockney acquired a few catchphrases from the French in the 1914-18 war. Inevitably, 'parly-voo' was one; it has more or less died out now, but a 'parlyvoo' meant a talking session, a confab. 'San fairy ann', for 'it doesn't matter', is still going strong. Two more were 'ally toot sweet', for 'get a move on', and 'napoo fini' for 'it's over'; the latter was used chiefly when something was broken. Neither is heard much today. In addition, men who had served in France like to show off with items such as 'Vooly-voo promade avec moi?' or, in a daring mood, 'vooly-voo cooshay avec moi?'

A word which may have come in from French is 'mush' for the face. The Romany 'mush' has always been used in the same way as 'mate', i.e. 'my good friend'. In this other sense, it is generally applied to the face as object for attack: 'he stopped one right in the mush'. The origin may be *mouche* for the bull's-eye of a target. A non-French expression from the 1914-18 war is 'put the tin hat on' something. It means the same as 'crown': a final unwelcome touch, perhaps even a crushing blow.

The second world war did not add to the stock of foreign words, but it brought a few services' words into Cockney. 'Bullshit' has been made more intense and hostile. Originally it stood for window-dressing, humbug, and with this meaning survives as 'bull' in the services. In present-day Cockney language it means lies: 'don't give me all that bullshit!' = 'You're telling me a pack of lies'. 'A ballocking' is the standard term for a telling-off. It started life as 'chew [someone's] ballocks off', a severe reprimand, but was reduced to the essential by Cockneys; today it is possible to hear a boy say 'I've just had a ballocking off my mum'. Another wartime term is 'the bloke'. This was the commander of a ship, but now means the person responsible or who has the say-so in any given situation.

~ ~

A number of Cockney words are Yiddish. They were learned by kids from Jewish kids, and picked up by adults from the Jewish trades-people and at work. In the 'twenties and 'thirties every true Englishman in Stepney knew that 'meshganab' was 'potty', a 'schnorrer' was someone on the earhole, and a 'gonoph' was a thief. 'Schmutter' has already been mentioned. When an East Ender backed an unsuccessful horse it was a 'stumer', a dud; as a result he was 'in stook', in financial trouble. In those circumstances he was a 'schlemiel' — the word means simpleton, but has come to mean 'silly bugger'.

All these words are still in use, and all Cockneys know 'muzeltov' for 'good luck'. In pre-war days there were a few Jewish comedians who got their laughs by caricaturing their race; they were invariably introduced by some bars of music to which the audience sang 'Ra-ra-ra-ra, muzeltov'. 'Schemozzle' is the favourite Cockney word for a disturbance or confusion. The Jewish children's word for a gentile is 'yock'. It means a fool, but derives from 'yog' which is 'goy' (gentile) backwards; in the change of sound the Jews get a bit of their own back. In recent years 'schmock' has come into use as a knockabout term meaning 'silly ass' — often by people who do not know that it is an obscenity.

The early American talkies had an influence for a few years, specially on the young, and specially the language of gangster films. In the early 'thirties all the herberts went about saying 'Oh yeah', 'sez you' and 'scram'. They threatened to bump off those wise guys in the next street, and take them for a ride or put them on the spot. They were wise to the fact that Cagney didn't belong in Sing Sing — he'd been framed, some other big shot had pulled a fast one on him. 'Oh yeah' and 'sez me' died out when the talkies lost their novelty, but 'you're telling me' has become part of the language.

Various occupations had their own slang, and some of it filtered through to the rest of the community. 'Sling your hook', for 'go away', was supposed to have been butchers' slang. Butchers were also associated with back-slang, and some of them — particularly in bigger shops like Sainsbury's, where breezy young men were employed — cultivated it as a private language. Besides 'revil', 'yendiks', 'tibbar', peesh' and so on they had 'gib-eeno' for 'big one', 'taf' for fat, 'dlo' (pronounced 'dee-lo') for old and a good many more, including 'slabs' for the testicles. But 'yob' for boy and 'exis' for six have been in general use throughout this century. 'Yob' is often expanded to 'yobbo' for a larrikin, and 'elrig' for a girl used to be heard sometimes.

The dockers had a language of their own but mostly kept it to themselves. 'Perm' was fairly well known, for a permanent as against a casual employee. One of their words was 'greenacre', which meant goods falling out of a sling and so was used as a cry of warning like 'Look out!' Another word for 'mind out' that is still used by older Cockneys is 'billo'. It was originally 'Below!' shouted as a warning when something fell from a height, and presumably came from dockland; on building sites men call 'Under!' in the same circumstances. The word for 'look out' used by children in the 'twenties and 'thirties was 'weeny'. When they were getting up to mischief the smallest one of the group was always delegated to 'keep weeny'.

Commerce meant tradesmen and dealers coming into the East End and adding to the language from their specialist vocabularies. They also took some out. The slang of the fairgrounds has a lot of Cockney in it, and Cockney likewise has terms from fairground language. The mock auctioneers from the fairs often had stalls in London markets, while costermongers who were down on their luck would frequently get jobs in fairs. The two groups also mingled at race meetings, Derby Day in particular. Some went for pleasure and some on business. Many costers sought to earn extra money by selling racing cards and programmes, and they met and mixed with the auctioneers and grafters who were doing the same thing.

Gypsies were part of the fairgrounds. Besides tellng fortunes they ran the latrines — according to my father they would bawl at the tops of their voices: 'Accommodation! A piddle and a poop for a penny!' As these groups intermingled, slang passed from one to another and expressions which were common to Cockneys gained slight variations when they were used by the grafters. 'Grafters', incidentally, means hard workers in Cockney, but in its original form it meant men who worked lines in markets and fairs.

There is a full account of fairground slang in Philip Allingham's book *Cheapjack*, published in 1934. Here is a list of terms which ran between it and the Cockney language.

Barney: a fight or noisy quarrel. Other Cockney expressions for a fight are 'a dust-up', 'a bundle' and 'a shindy'. 'An up-and-a-downer' means a dispute, particularly a domestic one

Bevvy: a drink. In fairgrounds and circuses a heavy drinker is 'a bevvy merchant'

Bogey: a person who interferes with one's pitch or spoils one's game. In Cockney usage it is, of course, a copper

Bottle, as in 'not much bottle' or 'no bottle': no good. It can also be put in question form: 'Any bottle?' meaning 'Any good?'

Brassnail: a prostitute

Bunce: profit, or money made over and above what has to be accounted for

Chavvy (Romany): a child

Clobber: clothes (Yiddish)

Crackers: mad

Dooks or dukes: hands

Flim: a five-pound note, from the pre-war fivers which were big pieces of flimsy paper

Gaff: a fair or market. In Cockney, a gaff is an unspecified place, e.g. 'What's this gaff like?' Early versions of the music halls were called 'penny gaffs'

Gaffer: the fairground master. To Cockneys, any boss is 'the gaffer'

Gear: a grafter's stock. In the past it had the same meaning in Cockney, but it has been narrowed down to mean equipment and, later, clothing

Gelt: money. The majority of the mock auctioneers were Jews, so Yiddish terms were common to both groups

Gezumph (Yiddish): to swindle. In recent years the word has achieved a wider circulation to mean unethical outbidding in the house-buying market

Homey: a man

Jam jar: a car (rhyming slang)

Kip: a bed or sleep — 'Where can I get a kip for the night?' or 'going to get some kip'

Lark: a line of business

Fanny: a grafter's sales patter. Cockneys use 'spinning a fanny' for telling the tale

Flash: a grafter's display, e.g. 'That's a good flash'

Moll: a woman

Mug faker: a camera

Mungary: food. Compare with 'manger'

Mush: friend, as a form of address — 'All right, mush?'. It is used by the gypsies in George Borrow's novels

Phunt (Yiddish): a pound

Pucker (Romany): to talk

Rosy: tea (rhyming slang, short for Rosy Lea)

RO: in fairgrounds, a fake auction: the initials are for 'run out'. To Cockneys the RO has always been the bunhouse or Relieving Office, and the Social Security office is still referred to by this name. It was also 'down below' — 'I'm going down below to get my money'.

Scarper: to run away, decamp

Screw: to look at

The smoke: London, and elsewhere in Britain the regional big city

Spiel (Yiddish): to talk or hold forth. Also a noun, e.g. 'He gave a long spiel'

Splits: the police. In Cockney it means plain-clothes men

Titfer: hat (rhyming slang)

Wide: knowing, has got his wits about him. After nearly a century's use in markets and fairs it became a common term in the late nineteen-forties in the phrase 'wide boy' for one who was a mixture of parasite and swindler

Donah: a woman. A Cockney song says 'Liza, you are my donah'

Burster: to do or have a burster is to do well and have good takings — the fairground or tent full to bursting point

Cushy, for 'soft' or 'easy', is probably Romany from 'kushto' (good); though an alternative explanation is the Hindustani 'khush', pleasure

Tanner for sixpence was discovered by George Borrow in use among the stallholders on London Bridge, and in *Lavengro* (published in 1851) he identifies it with the Romany 'tawno', the term for the smallest child in a family

Cock and hen: ten (rhyming slang)

Fly-pitching: unlicenced street trading; a term of the last forty years, since licencing systems were enforced by municipalities

Half a bar for ten shillings became current in the 'forties, but 'a bar' has never been used for a pound: it was always a quid, etc.

Gypsies are generally called 'gyppos'. However, both on fairgrounds and in Cockney talk a careful distinction is made between them and (often Irish) wandering caravan dwellers who are called 'diddikais', from a Romany word. Until fairly recent years there were a few small colonies of gypsies on the outskirts of East London, remnants of larger numbers who were prohibited from living in Epping Forest after it was taken over as a public park in 1878. Most of them are now in council houses. Gypsies are still regarded nervously, but it is widely believed that the women have special powers and to have one's fortune told by one of them is a great thing.

CHAPTER 4

Pure Vulgarity

The lav has always provided a lot of Cockney humour and imagery. The reason is not that Cockneys are innately coarse, but that living conditions have put the subject under their noses. In that circumstance, the choice is between pretending to be oblivious and getting some amusement out of it. Dean Swift did the same in satirical poems about upper-class connubiality amid chamberpots in the 18th century:

> How great a change, how quickly made!
> They learn to call a spade a spade.

'Lav' was a reasonably polite word for family use. So was 'w', short for 'w.c.' The latter was also abbreviated to 'dubs' by children. 'Closet' was just outside the edge of respectability; the word was harmless in itself but had an earthy sound. Some people referred to the place as 'out the back' instead of giving it a name. One term which was always thought objectionable was 'khazi'. It was brought home by foreign-serving soldiers, and it is hard to see why people were down on it — perhaps they thought it meant something terrible.

And, of course, there were the crude functional words like 'shithouse'. Soon after the end of the war a French football team played at Tottenham, and notices were put up for the visiting supporters; gazing at 'Pour les Messieurs', a man said to me 'That's French for pisshole, is it?' These words were (and are) also used as epithets carrying a special meaning. To call someone a closet, a shithouse or a pisshole states that he is thoroughly unprincipled and untrustworthy.

~ ~

In all working-class houses built before 1914 the lav was out the back, situated behind the kitchen for economical plumbing. Visits to it were conspicuous from start to finish. A person had to leave the house, ensuring that he had a supply of paper; at night-time there might be extra commotion because of the dark. The board door did not lend

itself to quiet opening and bolting. Entrances to and departures from
the lav could be heard or seen (probably both) by the neighbours at one
side, and they would keep an eye on it if they wanted to speak about
something. The next-door one at the other side backed on, and
simultaneous occupants could hear each other (they often called out
conversationally).

At the conclusion there was a noisy old-iron clank as the chain was
pulled, followed by a roaring which reverberated through the house for
at least two minutes — mains water filling the cistern via pipes under
the floorboards and round the kitchen walls. By the time the person
re-entered the house, everyone knew all about him. A high proportion
of families shared houses, which meant that they also shared lavs and
were obliged to be conscious of one another's physical functions.

Toilet paper was a luxury unknown to working people before 1939.
The common type of lav seat was a kind of wooden bench with a hole,
fitted to three walls of the little building. It was very comfortable; there
was space to put your coat at one side, and a couple of newspapers were
kept at the other side. You simply tore off pieces of them as required,
and came across interesting things to read. As a boy I was taken on a
visit to an aunt who lived in a semi-detached house a long way from the
East End. Her lav was out the back, but she had neat squares of
newspaper threaded on a string and hung from a nail on the door. I
thought this was elegant, a real sign of a higher way of life.

Because of the impossibility of privacy, the lav was a common
denominator: dignity and pretence were demolished by it. 'She thinks
her shit don't stink' is the classic phrase for a supercilious person. It is
fairly significant that the words 'shit' and 'crap' are both used also for
unpleasant or useless things. 'A load of crap' means contemptible
rubbish. Sometimes it is just the one word, as in 'That singer is crap'. In
recent times 'Shit!' has become fashionable as an exclamation of
annoyance. It was used by Cockneys fifty years ago, mostly in the fuller
form 'Oh, shit on it!' The only rhyming slang expression is 'tom-tit'.
Occasionally 'tish' is used — backslang — and the permitted word for
small children is 'poop', which can also be a near-genteelism.

Various beliefs about the workings of the bowels have added to the
range of humour and expressive phraseology. Everyone knew that
'regularity' had to be secured at all costs. Children who missed out were
kept home from school and given 'opening medicine', and adults would
take laxatives at once. The saying 'go through [something] like a dose of
salts' sums up the effects: swift and devastating. Posters for Kruschen
salts depicted a man full of *joie de vivre* leaping over a five-barred gate,

and a well-known quack doctor in the East End markets used to say: 'Of *course* he jumps over the gate! He hasn't *time* to stop and open it!'

What is now called a 'stomach upset' was funny (except to the one who had it) because of the disarray it caused. He was 'taken short', seized with a sudden imperative need which threatened utter disgrace if he did not get to the lav speedily: a wild rush through the back door, and consternation if the place was already occupied. Someone in this condition was said to have 'the runs', and might say he 'couldn't trust his arse with a fart'. A great, cruel practical joke was to put liquorice powder in a person's beer in a pub; it was a strong purgative which acted in a short time, so the jokers could see their victim's urgent runs. He was caused to 'shit blue lights' or 'shit through the eye of a needle'.

All this has provided metaphors for use in other connections. 'In the shit' means in deep trouble; it is a reminder of middens. A person who hangs on tight to some possession (or obsession) is 'sticking to it like shit to a blanket'. To have a piece of good fortune is to be 'shit-lucky'. This is said to come from a tradition that to be caught by a bird's dropping presages good luck; but there is 'arsehole lucky' as well, probably a pun on 'oh, so lucky'. Someone abysmally ignorant 'doesn't know shit from clay', and 'not worth a pinch of cold shit' means of no use to man or beast. Another declaration of worthlessness is 'I've shit 'em'. A person looking particularly miserable on a cold day is likely to be told that he resembles a frozen turd.

The decisive expression of rejection of something is 'Stick it up your arse'. Fewer people know George R. Sims's poem 'In the Workhouse' than know the Cockney parody of it.

> Up spoke the oldest pauper
> In a voice as bold as brass:
> 'We don't want your Christmas pudding —
> Stick it . . . '

A variation which is no politer but avoids the word itself is 'Stick it where the monkey sticks his nuts' (is not this a slander on monkeys?). 'Up yours', which is obviously short for the same thing, is an insulting rebuff; essentially, it means 'go to hell'. All references to the anus convey contempt. 'Arseholes!' is an answer in itself, the emphatic final word. A sycophant is an 'arsehole crawler'; presumably people who say 'crawler' for this do not know it is an abbreviation.

The fart remains something of a taboo. It makes Cockneys laugh, but to do it or laugh at it in public is generally thought indecent. The usual term is 'blow off' or, among children, 'let off'. However, it appears quite often in slang metaphors, usually in a way which represents the fart as a fuss about nothing (in the same spirit as the lavatory-wall rhyme 'Here I sit broken-hearted, Paid a penny and only farted'). Thus, to dither inconsequentially is to 'fart about' (sometimes 'fart-arse'). Anything unexpectedly and disappointingly small is a 'farting little' thing. When a person says he does not give (i.e. care) a fart he is indicating complete unconcern. Someone bustling or fidgeting to and fro is said to be 'in and out like a fart in a colander'.

It is the loud fart that causes amusement. Older Cockneys sometimes vindicate it with a country tag handed down from their grandparents: 'Where'er you be, Let your wind go free' (a later addition says 'Church or chapel, Let it rattle'). A man who farts persistently is said to have 'a farting clapper'. The noiseless, pungent fart is considered a dirty trick; it may cause sniggers, but more often rouses genuine disgust. Though nobody is deceived, the offender may try to blame his accuser by saying 'Your nose is too near your arse' or 'Foxes always smell their own holes first'. Certain foods, baked beans most of all, have the reputation of causing those who eat them to fart a great deal. A Cockney who has put down an opponent in argument often says triumphantly: 'That's stopped his farting in church.'

The other function is a 'Jimmy Riddle', a 'leak', a 'you and me' (rhyming for 'pee'); or 'sip', noun or verb, which is 'piss' backwards. 'Slash' came into use in the nineteen-forties and is still popular: 'Back in a minute, I'm going to have a slash.' Cockney women often say 'I'm going to strain my greens' — a truly ingenious piece of imagery. When Marie Lloyd was told to remove the line 'She sits among the cabbages and peas' from one of her songs, she substituted 'She sits among the lettuces and leeks'.

A man anxious to relieve himself will say 'I'm breaking my neck for a piss', and afterwards: 'I pissed buckets.' 'Pissing down with rain' is another common remark. Urine is usually made a symbol of weakness and unpleasantness, as in the expressions about tea (beer too). An ineffective football team, a bad film, etc., may be called 'piss-poor' or 'poor as piss' — 'and twice as nasty' is added in suitable cases. A person who shows off is described as 'all wind and piss'.

The pisspot has to be mentioned: the round, sturdy porcelain receptacle formerly kept under nearly every bed. Who wouldn't keep one for night-time use when the lav is downstairs, outside, dark and cold? By and in front of women and children it was called the po, the jerry or the chamber. In the early years of radio the BBC broadcast a lot of chamber music; not caring for it, Cockneys re-named it 'pisspot music'. A practice which was frowned on, seldom admitted, but widely practised by men was leaking in the kitchen sink if the lav was occupied (one might be surprised at the number of women who did it too). In fact the trendy modern urinal in the form of a thigh-high basin reminds me irresistibly of the kitchen sink.

There are countless jokes on these themes. Some are dreadfully unfunny, but others contain observation and wit: for instance, the man down the sewer who says 'With all the laxatives people use nowadays, you can't find a decent turd to stand your candle on'. Constipation, diarrhoea, farts and leaks have provided more mirth than any other subject. Rabelais, Marguerite of Navarre, Chaucer and Benjamin Franklin used the same humour for the same reasons. As sanitary conditions improved it was rejected by 'polite' society, but it remained alive among Cockneys because until recent years their sanitary conditions still had much in common with the Middle Ages. Younger Cockneys are less prone to lav humour, because in council flats with better amenities they do not have the matter insistently drawn to their attention.

Lav humour may also be a safety valve for some people. It is impossible not to notice that a lot of those who fall about at it are puritanical in other respects. A man who is embarrassed by any reference to sex and birth roars with laughter at the joke about the woman who used lead pellets as cake decorations and then shot the cat. Interest in the body's functions is natural enough; if he is shy over some of them, he may make up for it with the rest. The Cockney of comedy and romance is hearty and uninhibited. In real life he has his hang-ups like everyone else — and, as with his housing and plumbing, these are supplied to him by the society in which he lives.

~ ~

William Hazlitt wrote: 'The English, it must be owned, are rather a foul-mouthed nation.' Some years ago this was used in a magazine as a caption to a photograph of Billingsgate Market fishporters. Thus the point was made that *some* of the English are like that. Which ones? Cockneys, of course.

At that time, in the 'fifties, it was in the familiar tradition of tittering at the lower orders. The same thing came from pre-war thriller writers and wartime films: a few 'bloodys' and a 'bastard', a belch or two combined with comic-book illiteracy, and you had the Cockney depicted. Since then a new movement has arisen, particularly in the leftish theatre, to show the lives and struggles of working people as they really are. With a licence to use actual 'language' instead of merely hinting at it or giving spaced-out samples as in the past, the result — the supposedly pro-proletariat picture — is a Cockney who is more foul-mouthed than ever.

The issue is not whether Cockneys use swear-words and vulgarities copiously, because of course they do, but when and how. In fact there is a strong sense of propriety over them. To give examples, in a play about dockers in the 'twenties a man says 'Piss off!' in the presence of his young daughter; in another, a working man tells his family he is 'going for a piss'. Both of these are unthinkable. 'Piss off' was considered an insult (if it was not, the famous line in *The Virginian* applied: 'When you call me that, smile.') Normally it belonged to a quarrel, and even then only an exceptionally low person would say it in front of women and girls; his unmarried daughter's presence would make an absolute taboo.

This is still generally the case today. 'Emancipated' middle-class people probably swear less in total than Cockneys — the fact that they do not, on the whole, do hard physical work is one reason — but they eff and blind more indoors and between the sexes. A Cockney may say 'going for a piss', though he is likelier to use one of the other words, among his male workmates; in his home or in front of women he uses euphemisms. The staid ones are 'going out the back' (in more modern dwellings it is probably 'upstairs'), 'paying a visit', 'going to see a man about a dog' or 'be back in a minute'; women say 'I'm going to see my aunt'. Fruitier allusions are probably the outcome of mild embarrass-ment, feeling the need to make a joke about it, but they remain euphemisms. A man says he is going to pay his respects, or ease his mind, or sit on the throne; a bit more daringly, he is about to shake hands with an old friend.

Direct words for the bodily functions are usually avoided in any case. Women say that their children are 'loose' or 'bound' rather than that they have diarrhoea or constipation. With only one lav to a house, when someone occupies it for an extra-long time the others say he must have fallen down the hole, or that he wants a Number Nine (a terrifying purgative formerly given to soldiers). If a person with problems says he has not *been* for a week, it is unnecessary to add where — the one word is enough.

The words become permissible, subject to occasion and company, when they are in quips and sayings about other things. The referee at a football match 'must have shit in his eyes, he can't see straight'; or it is said of an immature person's opinions 'What does he know? He hasn't done shitting yellow'. A stock answer to a child's or an adult's excessive questions about food — what there will be, what is in it, etc. — is 'shit and sugar'. Women may and do say this within the family. They may also use lav words in nicknames, such as 'Fanny Fart' for a hoity-toity person (my father's version was the respectable 'Nancy Treadlight'). A common reply to banter is 'I'm not here to be laughed at, chaffed at or farted at'; this is good-humoured, not hostile, but it implies a warning.

'Arse' is one of the most widely-used words in the East End vocabulary (the Yiddish is 'tukas'). 'He's a nosy bugger, he wants to know the ins and outs of a cat's arsehole.' 'He's a cheeky young sod, he's got too much of what the cat licks its arse with.' Quite often in the past, when the landlord called for the Duke of Kent someone would say: 'I can't pay him today, he'll have to cork his arsehole up' (i.e. go without). One of the attractions of 'Khyber' as a rhyming synonym is the additional humour of 'up the Khyber Pass'.

Of a not-too-agile person it is said: 'Talk about slow! He wants a squib up his arse.' For the man who has got on in the world and become greedy in the process: 'Since he's come into money he doesn't know where his arse hangs.' An undersized person is called 'short-arse' if he or she is unpopular, 'shorthouse' as a more cordial form. Another reference to shortness is 'duck's disease', the explanation of which is 'your arse is too near the ground'. 'Arse' is not bad language, but it is an adults' word; the term for children and sensitive persons is 'bum'. Of course boys use it among themselves all the time, and to say it publicly is rather like one's first packet of cigarettes, a sign of growing up.

The distinction is made consciously between vulgarity and obscenity. Cockneys enjoy vulgarity. Apart from the fact that it can be funny, it is something distilled from the unasked-for conditions of East London life — a 'damn your eyes!' at the conditions and those responsible for (or complaisant towards) them. Obscenity has no such background; it is repellent because it is gratuitous — the commonest rebuke for it is that it is 'unnecessary', and it is felt to be justified only by anger or some other extremity. The foul-mouthed are considered low-class, and the East Ender resents that idea of him. He feels himself to be, and mostly is, a decent respectable citizen. A lot of Cockneys are polite in their speech specially to prove that point.

~ ~

Swear-words have several applications and types of meaning among Cockneys. The commonest is the use of one word as a universal adjective and adverb; it is intended to intensify what is said but becomes meaningless through over-use. A person addicted to this might say 'You'll never bleedin' believe it, but the bleedin' gaffer came up in his bleedin' car and told me and my mate to go back down the bleedin' yard, so we had to pack up our bleedin' things and bleedin' carry them, just because he can't bleedin' make up his mind . . .'

Forty years ago the adverb would have been 'bleedin' well' in each case, but the shortened form is standard usage now. 'Bleeding' has always been regarded as the strongest swear-word apart from the sexual words. Today 'fucking' often replaces it in utterances like the above, but this is for male company or else it is thought low (and in male company that sort of excessive use of the word may still be disliked). 'Bleeding' is best described as a single-sex word. Men use it among themselves, so do a good many women; but, generally, only distress or strong feeling justifies it between the sexes.

However, the swear-words are not just for vehemence. Taking 'bugger' as the example, because it is not considered foul and is freely used, the word expresses a variety of things. A bugger is a bad person: 'You bugger!' is, unmistakably, 'What a swine you are!' It is also a bad happening or situation: 'it's a bugger' is for something disagreeable or arduous. A person may say 'Bronchitis is a bugger, isn't it?' or 'The job I'm on is a real bugger'. As a verb it means the same. 'Bugger you' or 'bugger that' means to hell with you or it; 'buggered [up]' is damaged or finished off. 'Buggery' is perdition, as in 'go to buggery'; or 'all to buggery' for a hopeless condition.

A quite different note is struck when someone says 'poor bugger'. Here, the word carries strong compassion; and there is genuine good feeling in 'not a bad old bugger, is he?' or 'decent old bugger'. It may stand for persons in the same plight as oneself, e.g. 'They can get some other bugger to do that'. Addressed to children, it usually conveys affectionate amusement — 'look at that little bugger' — and this is extended to an adult who provides a pleasant surprise: 'Well, you young bugger!' 'Bugger me!' is an exclamation of light-hearted or feigned astonishment; 'well, I'm buggered!' is a bit more serious.

In these usages other swear-words are mostly interchangeable, but there are important degrees of intensity according to the words used. 'Bugger off' is a mild injunction; other terms (such as 'piss off') are both more forcible and more offensive. Likewise, 'bronchitis is a bleeder' goes further than calling it a bugger, and the strongest word of all would convey a tragic state. The scale of meaning can be illustrated from the term 'bugger-all' — a curious formation, but it has been in widespread use for forty years. To say 'nothing' or 'damn-all', the mildest form of this expression, is loose and unconvincing: 'I got damn-all' means I got something but am uninterested. 'Bugger-all' is stronger, and can be taken to mean 'little or nothing'. 'Sod-all' stands for a definite 'nothing'; and 'fuck-all' is a fierce, emphatic declaration — absolutely nothing and possibly less.

Blasphemy has always counted as swearing, to the extent that several substitutes are still used: for instance 'Gordon Brown!' or 'Gordon Bennett!' as genteelisms for the lower-class 'Gawd!' (Gordon Bennett was a well-known promoter of motor- and air-races before 1914. Any widely-known name may be taken by Cockneys for a slang purpose. The classic rhyming phrase for 'on one's own' is 'on my [your, his, etc.] Tod', from a popular American jockey at the beginning of this century named Tod Sloan. Later generations have used 'on one's Jack', short for Jack Jones. That might be anybody's name, but is probably the one who was an East London MP in the nineteen-twenties.)

The mildest irreligious exclamation is 'Blimey', and up to the last war children were still liable to be ticked off for using it — by parents who thought it was not nice, and by teachers or pious persons who would explain to the speaker that he was inviting the Almighty to strike him blind. A sophisticated grown-up version, in use then and now, is 'Gawd blind old Harry!' Its colourfulness conceals the fact that it is an evasion: naming a fictitious person to dodge consequences to oneself.

'Crikey' was more or less acceptable; so was 'Lor', pronounced 'law'. 'God' as distinct from 'Gawd' was an adult expression, usually meant to convey a serious arousal of feeling. Over many years, the commonest form of this has been 'Gor', short for 'Gorblimey' which faded away through a combination of disapproval and excessive use. Children said 'Corblimey' in the belief that the change made it all right; and this survives in the supremely expressive juvenile 'Cor!' (it has even been the name of a comic paper). 'Christ', however, was a bad swear-word. For a child to say it produced the same effect as 'bastard' or one of the sexual words: 'I'll tell your mum what you said, you see if I don't!'

A man who said 'Christ almighty!' or 'Jesus Christ!' in front of women was nasty; women who used them devalued their sex. Any condemnation of the Almighty, such as a desperate person might make, or a scurrilous joke about a religious matter was 'wicked'. Of course all this has altered in recent years. Blasphemies are used carelessly in public, like obscenities. Nevertheless, the two are ranked together, as in the phrase 'effing and blinding'; it is an indecent way of talking, for respectable people to shun.

Obviously this represents social custom in general, not confined to Cockneys. However, East Londoners have a special regard for the effect of words. Swearing, where it is not justified, produces cries of 'Mind your language', or just 'Language!'; 'Go and wash your mouth out' for the person using obscene words, and 'Don't be so bleedin'' wicked!' for the blasphemer. It does not come from any specially reverent feeling. The majority of Cockneys are apathetic or cynical towards religion, disposed to think that the clergy are 'always holding their hand out'. Probably the strongest reason is a determination to keep up standards of behaviour, combined with the wish not to risk celestial displeasure when things are already bad enough.

~ ~

Most Cockneys enjoy dirty jokes. They like jokes of all sorts — telling them is almost a dramatic art, and stories about sex have various functions. Among children, who start hearing them interspersed with lav jokes at about eight years old, they are a method of acquiring and passing on knowledge. Words previously known only as very bad swearing are shown to have meanings, and the tellers of the jokes are ready to give explanations in as much detail as they know. The result is a patchy but useful sex education. Its chief disadvantage is that it leaves young people wondering how much is true and how much is fiction or distortion; indeed, jokes keep sexual myths alive.

Another reason for the popularity of dirty jokes is that sex, like the lav, is seen as a great leveller. 'It takes away the dignity', a woman said to me in a factory. 'You see the Archbishop of Canterbury in his robes and then think of him puffing on top of his wife: of course it's funny!' A lot of jokes are about clergymen and nuns; an aristocratic scandal or, most of all, a royal wedding lets loose a stream of them. The Abdication period in 1937 produced jokes for months. East End children shrieked to one another: 'Why are Mrs Simpson's drawers like the flag on Buckingham Palace? Because they go up and down at the King's command!' while adults had more sophisticated versions. Underlying them was the thought of 'the Colonel's lady and Judy O'Grady': these people are as base as we are.

It is a leveller personally as well as socially. Jokes depict common plights: embarrassments, makeshifts, consequences of impatience or inexperience. They raise laughs precisely because everyone knows the situations which can arise from lack of privacy and with working-class family backgrounds. To other people the humour might appear as mere crudity, if it is not incomprehensible. In a community where Sunday Schools used to flourish because sending the children off to them gave the parents in a crowded home their only opportunity for intercourse, the laughter springs from recognition. There is an old joke (it would no longer be considered dirty) in which a girl waits to be alone with her grandfather and says 'Grandad, I'm in the family way', and he replies:

'Wait till you're my age — you'll be in everybody's way.' It is a Cockney life-story in two sentences.

CHAPTER 5

Social Questions

The Cockney does not have to define class — it defines him. While East Londoners are conditioned by the social system as are all other working people, they are resentful of it in a resigned sort of way and strongly conscious of 'Them and Us'. Parts of the East End which have always been deprived now share in the decay of the inner cities, with industries (the docks in particular) closing or moving out. In other parts the planners have created a new kind of desolation with modern amenities. Cockneys know that they are victims.

Thus, speaking well — 'talking posh' — does not make a great impression; it smacks of being the enemy's language. Nor are Cockneys taken in by showbiz personalities (and leaders in other fields) who, having long ago cleared off to higher-class surroundings, trade on their East End origins. Nobody begrudges their success or their opulence; but it is no use them pretending that they still belong, for they don't. This is not to say that being well-spoken causes hostility. It depends on whether the speaker is a 'lady' or a 'gentleman' in the true Cockney sense. A posh person who makes a favourable impression may be described as 'very select' (the word used to be seen on posters: 'A Select Dance', meaning no riff-raff).

Class is seen as a matter of functions and attitudes rather than of money. An East Ender who attains the big-car kind of opulence — it would once have been unimaginable, but has happened in the last twenty years — remains working-class by his own identification. On the other hand, people with modest incomes who fulfil an ambition to move to more genteel suburbs become 'lower middle class'. A rent- or debt-collector, petty official, etc., may be poorly paid and threadbare, but the idea that he is working-class is inadmissible: he is a representative of Them.

On this basis a standard of behaviour is clearly recognized. Cockneys are pleased when their children do well and head for living conditions better than theirs ever were, on the understanding that no social barrier is created by putting on 'superior' attitudes. Moreover, the criticism of somebody who does put on airs is likely to be: 'Who does he think he is? His old man only worked down the market, the same as mine.' But being 'common' is equally deprecated. Girls will reject styles of clothing, hair and make-up as common; the term covers bad manners, excessive familiarity and coarseness, demeanour in public, etc.

These things are related to 'self respect' by Cockneys. They mean good standing in the community, and underlying this is a strong working-class ethic. Social pretension is turning away from one's kind; commonness lets them down in another way, by confirming the worst things said about working people. What is and is not done varies a little between neighbourhoods and from street to street, but the broad framework is always there. If a young person starts associations which are disapproved of on these grounds, the advice to him or her is 'You can always stoop and pick up dirt'.

~ ~

East London has a reputation for patriotism. This rests chiefly on two things: wartime fortitude, and Cockneys' enthusiasm for royal processions and jamborees. In both there is a certain amount of willy-nillyness. Because of the docks and the concentration of industry, the East End was severely bombed. The Cockneys' virtue was to show a brave face and raise some humour, which they have always done against the tragedies and impositions of peacetime as well as wartime; and the press made the most of that, largely because of the risk that Cockneys might not want to go on living up to it. They were quite well aware, when chalking 'London can take it' on walls, that Hampstead and Surbiton were not the same London in that respect. A lot of the comicality, such as barbers putting up notices which said 'Hitler will be shaved free', expressed a fervent desire for the war to end.

At the beginning of this century a jubilee or a coronation was the only occasion when slum-dwellers were allowed in the West End. It was also possibly their only glimpse of pomp and pageantry, remembered for the rest of many a life, and this is reason enough for supporting royalty. To East Enders an anti-royalist is someone who wants to take away rare opportunities for a knees-up or a ding-dong. The monarchy gives a good show, and Cockneys like that. It is the same with weddings, and an undertaker who lays on solemnity with a trowel is said to 'give you a good show' (another phrase for a well-staged funeral is 'a lovely send-off'). Whoever deprecates this view of royalty should consider (a) that radicals and atheists practically all keep Christmas on the same principle of any excuse for conviviality, and (b) to stop a source of emotional satisfaction, however undesirable, you must have something to put in its place.

It is certainly not true that Cockneys are notable patriots. In 1935 a British film actor who was in the matinee-idol class appeared on the stage of the Troxy, the super-cinema of Stepney, and took it on himself to make a flag-wagging speech; he was booed until he had to leave the stage. Nor are they admirers of the ruling class. Churchill was profoundly unpopular all over East London, and that did not alter nearly as much as it is supposed to have done in the war. The common wartime view was 'he's a good leader but not of our sort of people'; and when Churchill spoke at a victory celebration rally at Walthamstow Stadium in 1945, he was booed as he had been in East London twenty years before. The 19th-century Tichborne case made a piece of working-class folklore and was talked about by Cockneys up to 1939 — Datas the Memory Man, a music-hall turn, specialized in the details of it. What the case showed, in Cockneys' opinion, was how the ruling class and their supporters ganged up unscrupulously against a lower-class person who tried to get in on their money and privileges.

The Cockney is as much or as little a political animal as working men and women elsewhere. East London has been overwhelmingly pro-Labour since the first world war, and the pre-1914 European immigrants helped to create a deeper vein of radicalism. Besides the fact that the Tories were the traditional class enemy in politics, the labour movement appealed to Cockneys because it offered discourse, argument and a means to self-improvement through books and pamphlets. Today they are probably less interested in politics than they have ever been. They still vote Labour, but without great conviction and with a sense that their pre-war parody of 'The Red Flag' is too true to be funny any more:

> The working class can kiss my arse —
> I've got the foreman's job at last

followed by

> I'm out of work and on the dole,
> So stick the Red Flag up your hole.

~ ~

Cockneydom is an uneasily multi-racial society. Those who regard themselves as 'native' East Enders are mostly descendants of families which came in from Essex, Suffolk and Hertfordshire in the 19th century for work in the docks, factories and markets and on the railways. Some have an older East London lineage, and others represent the half-a-million Irish who poured into the riverside areas in the 1840s. In addition, there have always been other-coloured immigrants. Before the last war there was a well-establshed little Chinese colony in Limehouse, and a small number of black people. Lascar seamen were plentiful round the docks; and Sikhs who carried suitcases full of cheap haberdashery, bought in Shoreditch warehouses, to sell on doorsteps. The most conspicuous additions, however, have been the wave of Russian and Polish Jews between 1880 and 1900, and the influx of Pakistanis and Bengalis in the last twenty years.

A small minority of Cockneys are openly racist and have it in for Jews and coloureds. A larger number grumble about them but would not accept trying to harm them or drive them out 'now they're here'. The grumbling is mostly connected with grievances over Social Security, housing and so on. As mixing takes place, it gives way to the sentiment 'there's good and bad among all people'; this acknowledges progress in relationships while leaving room to criticize when the speaker feels like it. The fear of getting a lot of Asian immigrants in 'our' street is not racial hostility so much as unease when neighbours with whom one converses easily on the basis of a common background are replaced by families whose style makes a barrier. After a generation this softens a good deal. The second-generation black man has assimilated a lot of East End culture, and his teenage daughter talks pure Cockney.

By enlightened middle-class standards in which the wrong word is outrageous, practically all Cockneys are racist in their talk. They refer to black people as 'darkies' or 'niggers' ('nig' is only used contemptuously); all people from the Indian continent, and the Asians who have come from Kenya and Uganda, are 'Pakkys'. Jews are 'Jewboys', 'Yids' or 'four-by-twos' — an older word was 'sheeny'. A Jewish man working among gentiles is likely to be called 'Ikey', just as a Scot is 'Jock' and an Irishman 'Paddy'. Italians are 'Tallyarners', a free-and-easy rendering of 'Italianos'.

In fact it is doubtful if these are racist words. If they are, it ought to be offensive to call somebody 'Ginger' or 'Lofty'. Though there is a mild cruelty in some of them, as there is in many nicknames and epithets — calling a spectacled person 'Foureyes', for instance — they are simply descriptive tags which, in general, do not carry malice. The two words for black or brown people that conscious racists use are 'wog' and 'coon', and they are not used by the majority precisely because of that. Cockney kids have always called out 'Walla walla Jewboy', in the same way as they shout derisively at anyone whose appearance strikes them and who may provide a bit of sport by chasing them. It may not be nice; but it does not have the meaning attributed to it.

Cockneys like jokes about Jews and the supposed characteristics of various nationalities. About half the jokes told by schoolchildren begin 'There was an Englishman, an Irishman and a Scotchman'. In late adolescence the formula is often extended by 'and a Jew', and this means that the joke will end with some great stroke of shrewdness. The main source of Jewish jokes is Jews themselves, and racists disapprove of them and allege that they are propaganda. There is no real body of humour about black people — indeed, the older type of crude joke involving sexual myths about black men has largely disappeared as the result of familiarity with them.

The nicknames and jokes are part of the flow of East End folklore and help to make the terms on which different nationalities and races live cheek-by-jowl with, on the whole, not much trouble. To call a cash register 'Yiddisher piano' conveys the legend about the Jews, but an amused tolerance as well. Something of the sort appears in comments about 'Pakky colours' (usually bright pinks and blues) for painting houses; they imply recognition and back-handed acceptance of another culture. In a more gracious environment, better consummations might be wished. In East London, harsh-sounding banter expresses relationships which may be the best obtainable when the whole population is aware of life as a collection of struggles.

~ ~

Besides the comic-illiterate picture of Cockneys, there is another which shows the East End as an area thick with drunkenness, violence and crime. From one viewpoint it would be surprising if this were not so — poverty and degradation have that effect. Charles Booth, in *Life and Labour of the People of London* in the 1880s, provided a descriptive map on which districts housing 'the very lowest class — vicious, semi-criminal' were marked in black. Whitechapel and Bethnal Green had about a dozen black streets; the most notorious part was the Old Nichol area, the scene of Arthur Morrison's *A Child of the Jago*.

The question is not whether this was true, because of course it was, but whether it was characteristic. Sir Walter Besant in his *East London*, written less than twenty years later, said almost the opposite: the East End was 'not a city of slums, but of respectability'. Like Besant, Booth and his team were middle-class observers. Invaluable as their survey and statistics were to social reformers, their descriptions often only helped to perpetuate myths (for example, the condescending account of the Bow match girls). In the past as now, the East End had both respectability and crime. At all times, crime has involved only a small minority of the population.

The two things do not exclude each other. Most crime is thieving of one sort and another, and the fellows who do it are often respectable among their families and neighbours. Cockneys do not approve of it, for practical reasons more than moral ones: the attentions of the police can be done without. They do not say a man who gets into this kind of trouble is bad, but that he is 'silly'. Crimes against the person are a different matter, and generally are viewed with loathing; the Krays became known as 'wicked buggers' on that account only.

However, there has been a change of attitude over petty crime. Up to 1945 it was a golden rule that a tea-leaf did not do it on other working people — the well-to-do and shops and companies could 'spare it', i.e. stand the loss, but to rob one's own kind was despicable. That no longer applies, and the poor are vulnerable because they are skimpily protected (also because they do not expect it). As part of this change, community trust is no longer possible. Offences such as stealing milk from doorsteps rarely occurred because they were unthinkable in the past, but now are accepted likelihoods. A great many front doors had a loop of string attached to the inside part of the lock dangling behind the letter box, dispensing with the need for keys; you inserted your fingers, felt for it and pulled. That practice has completely disappeared.

The majority's disapproval of unprincipled thieving and resentment of other crimes are balanced by Cockney's dislike of 'the law'. Besides its normal meaning, the phrase is a name for policemen: 'the law was round here' = 'a policeman or some police came'. Cockneys as a whole share Aldous Huxley's sentiment that no civilized person would be a policeman: they regard it as a disgusting job, watching and telling on other people. They are not surprised by reports that police take bribes and beat people up — these have always been facts of life in East London — and take for granted that the legal apparatus supports the upper class and the haves against the have-nots.

From this point of view, 'the law' is only another sort of criminal, and the slang and nicknames for it are unaffectionate. No Cockney would use the cuddly-sounding 'bobby' or even 'bluebottle' for a policeman. 'Copper' remains the universal word, and sometimes 'flat' (short for flatfoot). 'Rozzer' is said mostly by children, and the American 'fuzz' has never got going among Cockneys. Recently 'old Bill' has come into use, and seems to be growing in popularity; it is used in the same way as 'the law', and is sometimes rendered as 'the old Bill'.

To nick something is to steal, of course, but 'the nick' is the police station. Other words for stealing are 'lift' and 'swipe', and these are plainly descriptions of physical actions. The development of 'cop' is interesting. Originally it meant to catch or capture; the Oxford Dictionary instances its use in 1704. 'Copper' for a policeman comes from that, and itself was abbreviated to 'cop'. However, this caused its meaning to be extended to include the idea of retribution. Cockney children said 'you won't half cop it', i.e. be punished, and in the 'thirties it became 'cop out', to receive one's deserts. In the last few years, perhaps through a misunderstanding of the term, 'cop out' has become non-Cockney for dodging out of something and is now used for a facile or evasive solution to a problem: e.g. 'that book has a cop-out at the end'. But the original meaning is still active in Cockney — 'cop this' means catch or grab hold of it.

A plain-clothes policeman or detective is a dick or a split. In the 'twenties and 'thirties when mounted police were used against unemployed demonstrations they were called Cossacks; usually, 'the bloody Cossacks'. Informers (the lowest of the low) are narks. To be arrested is to be pinched, nicked, get one's collar felt or be collared; but 'pinched' also means being charged with any offence. When that happens a person is 'had up', and if he goes or is taken to court he is 'up before the bench'. A habitual criminal who does not care what he does is a villain.

~ ~

There is less violence in the East End today than ever before, despite the present-day concern over mugging and hooliganism. Several factors are involved. In the past, in the toughest times, large numbers of families in East London actually saw little of fisticuffs or threatening behaviour. That is still true, but everyone now is aware of the dangers of being out alone at night.

This in turn reflects changed social conditions. Mugging and assault have thrived in the last twenty years on the streets being more or less empty at nights. Formerly they were well populated until midnight and after. The shops were open late; people went to visit friends and to cinemas and other amusements on foot instead of by car; there was a lot of standing-about outside or in the doorways of pubs, talking at corners and going for walks in the streets; children played in the side turnings. Compare that scene with the deserted approaches to blocks of flats, and the way main roads virtually die about half-past six every evening. In consequence, families are conscious of a danger which did not exist before and see it as an increase in violence.

Certainly East London had plenty of roughness in the past. It needs no explaining. Partly as cause and partly as effect, there was a strong tradition of masculinity; a man was expected to behave masterfully in and round his home, and show himself ready to throw his weight about. Realistically, one needed to be able to defend oneself. Boxing was the supreme sport in the East End. The professional boxing centres in the 'twenties were Premierland and Wonderland, and in the 'thirties the Devonshire Club at Hackney and Mile End Arena. There were (and are still) several amateur clubs, and most Cockney men have 'done a bit' at some time — the local papers give a substantial part of their weekly sports pages to boxing news. Outstanding boxers became folk-heroes; an important factor in improving the Jews' standing was the emergence of very good Jewish boxers.

Pugnacity comes into Cockney language a good deal. Several everyday expressions come direct from boxing, such as 'in a clinch', 'below the belt' and 'square up'. 'Having one's back to the wall' has more to do with street fighting. A disappointment or rebuff is 'a smack in the eye', and an injured or afflicted eye is always said to be 'bunged up' as if closed by somebody's fist. A crony is 'my old sparring partner'. A person uncertain about attempting something will decide or be urged to 'have a bash'. Shrewd evasion of problems is 'boxing clever'.

'Lay off', meaning stand back or desist, is a less obvious boxing reference: it is the inferred opposite of 'lay on', when a boxer leans his weight on the other man. (Children use the same construction in 'hang off', shouted to someone who is pulling or hanging on to them.) 'Belt', 'thump' and 'clobber' are all words for 'hit'; so is 'poke', but it is a more specific image of the boxer's jabbing arm. Another expression is to 'clock' somebody — e.g. 'I clocked him one': hit him in the clock or dial. It is said of a weak fighter that he 'can't box kippers' or 'couldn't punch a hole in a paper bag'.

The word 'tan', borrowed from the leather industry which used to flourish on the other side of Tower Bridge, also means to beat somebody: 'he tanned him', or 'I'll tan your backside'. Presumably 'a good hiding' is from the same source. But these terms are also used for having a wholehearted go at something — 'the kids have tanned that bag of cakes' or 'I gave that pile of work a good caning' means that big inroads were made.

The taken-for-granted violence implied in these words and phrases has fallen off dramatically in the last forty years. 'Caning' referred not only to school, where young children were often 'whaled' unmercifully, but to the small canes sold in oilshops for home use; and 'belt' also was quite literal. Men commonly wore broad leather belts and braces too, so that they could take off the belt and use it to thrash their children. It was assumed that practically any adult was licensed to give boys in particular a 'clump' or a 'clip round the earhole' (the threat was to give a boy 'a thick ear', i.e. the cauliflower ear seen on boxers who were badly beaten about the head).

Fights in the street were not uncommon, with a crowd of spectators urging the combatants on. The police were not anxious to notice them. At about nine years old I saw a furious struggle outside a pub and was sent to find a copper. I ran into one quickly; when I told him, he said 'If I was you, son, I'd go and look for a policeman' — and turned and strolled the other way. Sometimes fights between women were seen, and these were terrifying affairs. Male fights had to be 'fair' in terms of the rules for fist-fighting, though they usually ended in undignified wrestling and kicking, but women went for each other's hair and would use any weapon to hand.

How many men knocked their wives about is difficult to say. The safest answer is a sizeable minority; by the 'thirties a man who did it was badly thought of, but it is also true that most labouring men thought it was open to them to hit their wives if they felt provoked. Older people today often half-deride the concern over 'battered wives' by saying that within their memory half the wives in East London were battered. That was never so, but it indicates the change which has taken place. Though girls with black eyes can be seen waiting on police-court doorsteps in the mornings, personal brutality has now become an exception. The increase of violence in crime does not alter the fact.

~ ~

A lot of brawling is connected with drink. Jokes about fights are usually placed in pubs, as if that does away with the need for explanation. It is not just a question of being 'the worse for drink'; in a pub, many men feel themselves to be on their mettle and are almost on the look-out for any affront so as to show that they stand no nonsense.

At the beginning of this century drink was the outstanding social evil, not merely in the East End but all over Britain (as in the saying that the Guinness family were good to the poor of Dublin and the poor of Dublin were even more good to the Guinness family). There is a wealth of descriptive evidence from observers — Seebohm Rowntree in 1903 estimated that one-sixth of working-class families' incomes, on average, went on drink. True as all this may be, it gives a distorted picture of East London as a whole. A large part of the population drank moderately or not at all; they knew they could not afford it, and looked on boozing with distaste. The Jews despised the gentiles on account of drinking.

In fact the observers all had interests in making the picture as black as possible. Radicals did so because the Conservative Party, which dominated government in Britain for twenty years, was virtually owned by brewers. For the middle-class charity-mongers drink was a stick to separate the undeserving from the deserving poor, and it provided the diehard legend that if working people are given money they only booze it away. Others were so intrigued or horrified by what they saw that they over-generalized. An example of this is in Eileen Baillie's book *The Shabby Paradise*, recalling Poplar as seen by a small child in a vicarage before 1914. Describing the pubs, she mentions women urinating in the gutter while standing talking outside them.

Presumably she saw it happen and was so fascinated as to make it a universal practice — 'they had a habit' of it. Cockney women whose mothers belonged to that generation would refute this and say that the 'habit' was inconceivable except among a small, low minority. Likewise, older Cockneys used to recall the Salvation Army holding meetings outside pubs and the customers sitting on the kerb singing the hymns with pints in their hands; but the fact that they noted and were amused by it means that they themselves did not lead that sort of life.

Most Cockneys like a drink, within their means. The modes of it have altered a good deal. The pub has always functioned largely as the centre of community, where people got together in numbers on free-and-easy terms. On the other hand, finances and the status of women made it more a male than a family gathering-place in the past; some men went out drinking to get away from their homes, and wives accompanied their husbands to pubs chiefly on Saturday nights and at holiday-times. These were the nights for sing-songs, sentimentality and quarrelling, and also when children stood on pub doorsteps (the common relief for a waiting child was an arrowroot biscuit, which was big and long-lasting).

Up to 1939 drinking meant beer, almost entirely. There was a lot of going out, or sending children, to fetch beer to drink indoors; many elderly people and women whose husbands were at work went to the off-licence with jugs at dinnertimes. If they drank stout, a common practice was to plunge a hot poker in it — this was said to 'bring out the iron' and do the drinker good. Men who were going through hard times would sometimes fall back on packets sold in herbalists' shops; mixed with water the stuff made a flat beer. There was little spirits-drinking, for obvious reasons. The opinion was often voiced that spirits 'are bad for you': as with men who said they preferred Woodbines or hand-rolled shag cigarettes, the argument was from necessity.

All this has changed in the last twenty-five years, through a combination of social factors. Drink remains a pleasure, a beverage and a foundation of social life to Cockneys. Since the first world war habitual drunkenness has been relatively uncommon in the East End, and most Cockneys associate it with being moneyed. Stories about drunks in the early-morning market pubs invariably concern toffs who have been out all night; between the wars a stage comedian named Jimmy James did a drunk act dressed in top hat, white tie and tails. That was the image. Nor was a working-class boozer necessarily a non-respectable person. Characteristically, he was the head of a family and his precepts were as firm as anyone else's.

What is noticeable about Cockneys' slang to do with drinking is its lack of affection or praise for the stuff. The terms are either euphemisms or contemptuous-sounding. 'Drink' is itself a euphemism: to say 'my father drinks' is conveying that he is a drunkard. The expressions proposing a drink — 'have half-a-pint', 'have a wet', 'a quick one' — are under-statements. 'Booze' is the almost universal verb and noun; 'boozer' is a pub, also a person who drinks heavily; a well-lubricated party is a 'booze-up'.

Words for drunk (besides 'boozed') are 'sozzled', 'tight' and 'pissed'. The last is the most common nowadays, its use having grown steadily from the late 'thirties; in male company it is often extended to 'pissed as a newt', 'pissed as arseholes', etc. Fairly inebriated is 'half cut', and thoroughly so is 'paralytic', short for 'paralytic drunk'. An older expression is 'blind drunk'. Often, someone making known that another is drunk does not speak at all: he opens his mouth and points into it with his forefinger. The evocative phrase 'drunk as a fiddler's bitch' has been thieved for middle-class usage, but it originated between London pubs and the fairgrounds in the 19th century.

Pub proprietors are referred to as publicans; unless specially friendly terms exist, an individual one is addressed as 'guv'nor' and spoken of as 'the guv'nor'. Generations of schoolchildren in London and elsewhere have been flummoxed by being told that publicans in the Bible are tax-gatherers; the more so because 'public-house keepers and sinners' would make sense but 'tax collectors and sinners' does not. The information is usually given in a way which implies that the children's vocabulary is at fault, whereas the opposite is true — the Bible 'publican' is a historical curiosity, but it has been established in the public-house meaning for at least two hundred years.

Some miscellaneous expressions: Gin is known as 'Mother's ruin'. 'Four-ale bar' means the public bar, where beer is cheaper than in the other bars — 'four' is short for 'fourpenny'. A gratuity given openly, as against the stealthier 'drop', is called 'beer money' or 'a drink' (like the French *pourboire*). The saying 'It's the beer talking' is given wrongly by Partridge. He has it as a public-house jocosity when somebody farts; in fact Cockneys say it about belligerence or bravado shown by a person who is half-cut. The standard remark when a drunken person falls and cannot get up is 'Mann and Crossman [or some other firm of brewers] holding you down'. Closing time is 'chucking-out time' — once a realistic enough phrase. This has become a general expression for the end of hours in any place, e.g. 'When is chucking-out time at the public library?'

Sing-songs still take place in some pubs, though the musical entertainment today is much more likely to be a rock group. A public holiday or a wedding is an occasion for a booze-up, and a lot of Cockney families visit pubs regularly. The difference between past and present is seen most clearly at Christmas, however. Walking along East End streets at night, the rows of houses are dark and still; a generation ago they resounded with 'Knees up, Mother Brown' and the thumping of pianos. Asked how they enjoyed Christmas, the majority of people say 'Very nice — quiet, you know'.

CHAPTER 6

Sally Broke the Jampot

In *Harry the Cockney,* published in 1912, Edwin Pugh described the typical Cockney as eloquent but not articulate. He was referring to East Londoners' reluctance to show their feelings, and their apparently scoffing attitude to emotional life. It must have irritated Pugh, for he said: 'But the spirit, the soul, of the Londoner is usually dumb.' Eloquent the Cockney certainly is, however. It would be a mistake to call his culture an oral one; it is a *verbal* culture — he (or she) enjoys words, written or spoken, and the possibilities they offer.

Because they delight in talking, Cockneys like to be well informed. They have always been keen readers of newspapers. In the last fifty years East London has never been without shops and stalls selling second-hand books; the stall in Chrisp Street, Poplar, before the last war dealt in excellent stuff and was attended by crowds. Several supposedly superior parts of Greater London have never supported a bookseller! There are many more contradictions to the idea of the illiterate East Ender of the past (never mind about the present). The ubiquitous boxing posters gave lengthy small-type details under every performer's name: 'A great two-handed fighter. Recently K.O. Bill Briggs in S. Area welterweight title eliminator', etc. In the music halls the words of songs were displayed on framed sheets so that everyone could sing them and commit the words to memory for future use. These and other practices show a communication-conscious culture of which reading was an essential part.

The music hall dealt largely with the enjoyment of words. Besides banter, puns, ripostes and irony, it affirmed the fun of versifying and phrase-making. The exhibitionistic nature of rhyming slang is part of this. So is the comic chorus chant — a man has only to utter opening words for all those round him to join in. For example:

Today being my daughter's wedding day,
A thousand pounds I'll give away.

(Cheers and cries of 'Good old squire!' 'One of the best!')
> On second thoughts, I think it best
> To keep it in the old oak chest.

(Groans, boos: 'Mouldy old squire', 'Tight-fisted sod', etc.)
Another is 'If you vant to buy a vatch, buy a vatch. If you don't vant to buy a vatch, take your snotty nose off my nice clean vindow!'

In the same vein, the audience at a political meeting may sing 'Tell me the old old story' if the speaker is platitudinous; or, if he tries an emotional appeal, mime violins playing drawn-out notes. This kind of thing can be heard at football matches — not the supporters' chants, but the communal enjoyment of an incident. A man has something happen to his eye, and is led to the first-aid post holding a dressing to the eye; twenty thousand people call out 'Aye aye!' as he passes in front of them. The trainer strokes a player's injured back, and a great mock-maternal 'Aaaaah!' goes up.

There is a vast legacy of phrases and lines from music-hall songs, and they are whipped out as often as they are appropriate. The scrap-dealer's cry 'Any old iron' was immortalized by Harry Champion's song and is called out to anyone with an old bike, an ailing car or the like. 'Ginger, you're barmy' and 'I see you've got your old brown hat on' were more Harry Champion. 'Coughing better' came from George Formby senior — a person who has a coughing fit must suffer either this remark or 'It isn't the cough that carries you off, It's the coffin they carries you off in'. 'Getting a big boy now', 'just to show there's no ill-feeling', 'one of the ruins that Cromwell knocked about a bit', 'where did you get that hat?', 'a little of what you fancy does you good', 'the likes of 'er', ''e dunno where 'e are', 'has anybody here seen Kelly?' and countless other stock sayings have the same origin.

A by-product of music-hall songs was phrases fitted to the instrumental flourishes between lines, and some of these have gone into wider use. 'Have a banana' came into being because it went with the five notes following the first line of 'Let's all go down the Strand'. It is invariably sung as part of the song now, and probably a lot of people believe the composer wrote those words as well; however, 'have a banana' has a life of its own as a faintly rude back-answer. 'How's your father? Blind drunk!' also fitted some well-known rounding-off notes, rather like 'Pom tiddly om pom, pom pom!' Presumably because it means nothing, 'how's your father' has become the phrase for anything a speaker does not want to be heard naming: for example, someone offering a surreptitious drop of whisky says 'Do you fancy a spot of how's your father?'

East End children are the heirs of this tradition, and revel in standing words on their heads and making them jump through hoops. Nursery rhymes quickly give place to verses embodying the humour of the streets. Parodies of other people's songs have always been a favourite amusement. In the 'twenties and 'thirties children chanted as they skipped:

Sally broke the jampot, and blamed it on to me.

The tune was 'The Keel Row'. A favourite Irish sentimental song got rougher treatment when they changed 'Come back to Erin, Mavourneen, Mavourneen' to:

Come back with hair on, you bald-headed bathbun.

However, a lot of the Cockney kids who sang that were of Irish descent. 'Bathbun' was a way of not-quite saying 'bastard'.

It is hard to see how bits of operatic tunes were learned — possibly they were played by the pit orchestras in the music halls. They were quickly given new words. 'La donna e mobile' took up a familiar theme vivaciously:

Ta ra ra boom de ay, we've had no grub today.

Been here since Sunday, come back on Monday.

The soldiers' chorus from *Faust* produced:

Oh Glory! look at your uncle Jim

He's in the duck pond teaching the ducks to swim.

Patriotic songs were insistently taught at school, and just as determinedly parodied. Making the tunes familiar was asking for this, of course, and the words were bound to be irreverent as in the schoolboys' version of 'The British Grenadiers':

There was a Scotch Highlander at the Battle of Waterloo.

The wind blew up his petticoat and showed his half-past two.

And:

Land of soapy water, mother wash thy feet,

Father cut thy toenails, put 'em on a plate to eat.

There was 'Rule Britannia, two tanners make a bob', and an obscene variation which began 'Rule Britannia, three monkeys up a stick'. Another skit, sung by adult males, was

A life on the ocean wave, afloat on the bounding deep,

We haven't got time for a shave, we haven't got time for a shit.

Not very witty, that one; its humour was mainly in the switch from the 'proper' words to improper ones and the surprise to a listener who had not heard it before. If a man sang anything like that indoors, his wife was bound to say 'Why don't you shut your bloody row — God forgive me for swearing!'

In a different field, there was: 'The Lord said unto Moses, Come forth! but he came fifth, and he lost his beer money.' And:

The Lord said unto Moses
All Jews shall have long noses,
Excepting Aaron — he shall have a square 'un,
Excepting Peter — he shall have a gas meter.

There was no anti-semitism in that: in children's rhymes everyone was fair game. Another skipping rhyme was

Salvation Army, all gone barmy,
All gone to heaven in a corned beef tin.

As often as not, the beginning was altered to 'Sally Sally Army'. The Boys' Brigade had fun poked at them in a verse which was half sung, half chanted to go with their drum-and-bugle band when they paraded through the streets:

Here comes the Boys' Brigade, all covered in marmalade,
With a twopenny-ha'penny pillbox and half a yard of braid.

There was no verse for the Boy Scouts — perhaps 'Brussel Sprouts' said it all.

Hymn tunes also were gratefully accepted. Besides being learned in school, they were heard when the Salvation Army bands played in the streets. General Booth was also the source of free tea and buns, and the children showed their gratitude by turning 'Stand up, stand up for Jesus' into

Sit down, sit down for Gawd's sake,
The people at the back can't see.

A sweet sentiment for small children was brought to earth:

Jesus wants me for a sunbeam
And a bleeding fine sunbeam am I.

Sometimes only a beginning was altered; presumably the creators ran out of ideas. A version of the National Anthem started 'Gawd save our old tom cat, Feed him on bread and fat' and then reverted to normal; and the hymn 'Holy, holy, sing to Mary' began 'Hallelujah, skin a donkey'. It seems a pity the latter was not finished; it had possibilities.

At some point 'fainits' must be mentioned. It is a key word in East End children's lore, and means 'truce'. If, during a game, a boy or girl wants to claim a temporary respite or the opponent to desist — for a visit to the lav, because clothes are damaged or for any other reason — 'fainits' compels it. The opponent may ask 'Why?' but must still honour the call; and it must not be used falsely. Other forms of it occur elsewhere, but 'fainits' is the definitive Cockney term.

Among chants and rhymes, the pretty songs and nationalistic poems taught in school provided much material. There were several versions of 'Casabianca', such as

> The boy stood on the burning deck
> With half a sausage round his neck,
> A squashed tomato in his eye —
> There he was, left to die.

That was comical nonsense, but another version alluded to bad habits:

> The boy stood on the burning deck
> Picking his nose like mad;
> He rolled it up in little balls
> And threw them at his dad.

A long poem about a heroic deed in the American Civil War (don't ask why this was taught in schools in the East End of London) had the lines 'Up the street came the rebel tread, Stonewall Jackson riding ahead'; that was rendered as 'Up the stairs came a heavy tread, Stonewall Jackson going to bed'. And a ditty called 'The Lass of Richmond Hill' had new words put to it:

> The lass of Richmond Hill
> She took a Beecham's Pill

— the remainder is rather coarse.

A lot of verses were scatological. Children's natural curiosity about the physical functions was partly responsible for this, but it combined with the knowlege that the lav was an acceptable subject for humour. Thus:

> In days of old, when knights were bold
> And paper wasn't invented,
> They wiped their arse upon the grass
> And went away contented.

And a version of 'Yankee Doodle Dandy':

> Mother Brown went to town
> To buy some macaroni.
> She let a fart behind a cart
> And paralysed the pony.

Another, which contained references to precepts about behaviour, has almost certainly been made obsolete by changes in dress:

> Ask no questions, tell no lies,
> Never see a Chinaman doing up his flies.

There were verses which seemed to have been handed down from one generation of schoolchildren to another, and their origins were unknown. For instance:

Sam, Sam, the dirty old man,
Washed his face in the frying pan,
Combed his hair on the leg of a chair
— Sam, Sam, the dirty old man.

And nonsense verses like this one:

I went round the straight crooked corner
To see a dead donkey die.
I took out my pistol to stab him
And he landed me one in the eye.

Though the past tense has been used, Cockney children use these and similar chants today. Many of them contain social satire; but what they demonstrate above all is a consciousness of word-play as fun, and this remains life-long.

~ ~

Humorous writers have often put malapropisms into East Enders' mouths. The intended joke is the idea of ignorance of the English language. Insofar as this is true at all, it applies to only a few; but deliberate malapropisms are a part of the private humour Cockneys enjoy.

Children invent them continually. Films in the 'thirties were re-named 'The Four Horsemen of the Eucalyptus' and 'Rice Pudding the Mad Monk'. Film stars became Marlene Dirt-Track and Deanna Dustbin; the other way round, macaroni was Mickey Rooney. Everyone know about the journey from Land's End to Quaker Oats, and It's a Long Way to Tickle Mary. The Italian beauty spot in a popular song was the Isle of Debris. Youths who could not afford Harlene or Brylcreme for their hair slicked it down with water and said they were using 'Tapolene'.

Adult examples are 'she-male' for female; 'I should cocoa' for 'I should hope so' said ironically — e.g., 'Go all that way for nothing? I should cocoa!'; 'testimonials' for testicles. (The last is partly a euphemism but is also a souvenir of an old joke which ends 'And I lost the job through sheer bloody ignorance!') But several established malapropisms have the flavour of words which ought to exist. An outstanding example is 'outdacious'. It is a cross between 'outrageous' and 'audacious', and conveys a shade of meaning for bold-as-brass cheekiness that neither of those words achieves. Another is 'confab', short for 'confabulate', which means a serious-faced conference: 'They're all in the office having a big confab'.

'Spiflicate', as in 'The missis will spiflicate me when I get home', is another word-mixture which fills a gap; it means a comprehensive good hiding. 'Crafty' is used for 'surreptitious' but extends its meaning; 'slip out for a crafty smoke' indicates the person's shrewdness in knowing when and how to get away with it. East End factory girls often accuse somebody of 'throwing out snacks'. It sounds like chucking sandwiches about, but a person doing this is casting innuendos. The word that 'snacks' misrepresents is hard to identify; it invokes 'sneer' and 'snide', or may be from 'sneak' — making sneaky remarks. Probably the best-known Cockney malapropism is 'hokey pokey' for ice cream. All experts agree that it came from 'hocus pocus', though it is hard to see what that had to do with ice cream. It meant specifically the stuff sold by Italians from barrows in the streets, before public health regulations condemned us to pale shadows of it.

Phrases as well as words are consciously misused to produce different effects. If a fellow inadvertently turns his back to his girl friend, she draws it to his attention by saying 'Nice to see you're [your] back again'. The same girl may say to her mate on Sunday evening: 'Let's go for a walk on a bus.' A prudent person lending something says 'Don't forget it's got a back to it': that is, be sure to return it. Another meaningful absurdity is 'You'll get your eye in a sling' = I will put one on you. I have heard a doctor ask 'How do you feel?' and his Cockney patient, poker-faced, reply: 'With my hands.'

No occasion for verbal amusement is missed. A strong smell is credited with extra impact on the senses: 'Don't half hum' or 'Doesn't half whistle'. A person who has stayed out late is greeted with the epithet 'nasty stop-out', and men who find that they are behind with what they have to do will cry 'Four o'clock and the baby's not been washed!' 'Do yourself a mischief' was once a serious warning but, probably because it is a clumsily sententious euphemism, has long been a bit of fun. It means to injure some very tender part — the sight of a fellow climbing a spiky fence, for instance, leads to the mention of 'a mischief'. Even the three brass balls over a pawnshop come in for humour: they are said to stand for 'two to one you don't get it back'.

Having a word for everything is not the same as making light of it. The belief that Cockneys laugh off troubles and tragedies is a chronic disadvantage to them. It has meant they are imposed upon and treated contemptuously: the East End will, supposedly, put up with anything. The Cockney knows this, and the knowledge produces a certain defensiveness. Besides being the centre of his culture, his verbal flow is his weapon.

~ ~

The logic of the language is masked continually by calculated perversities, under- and over-statements, and apparent contradictions. To the outsider it seems wayward and devoid of rules, and there is no Rosetta Stone. The most careful scholars, not Cockneys themselves, seldom fail to get hold of the wrong end of the stick — or, in East End language, arse upwards.

How are they to know about bogeys, for instance? It is a word for flats or coppers; it also means cakes of mucus in the nose. (To 'get up one's nose' is another matter: it means to annoy.) In addition, a bogey is a jinx or Jonah, as in 'Don't have him with us, he's a bogey and puts the mockers on things'. And consider 'one and a kick' for one-and-sixpence. That is straightforward enough, and so is 'two and a kick' for half a crown. Consistently, sixpence should be 'a kick' — but it is not. A trousers pocket is a kick, instead. That is a remnant of the old slang word for trousers, 'kicksies'; Arthur Morrison used it in *A Child of the Jago*, published in 1896, but it was probably out of date even then.

'Ta ta' is equally elusive. As a word for 'goodbye' it is too well known to need explanation, but 'coming ta-tas' means togetherness instead of parting: it is what a mother says when proposing to take a small child out for a walk. If she is sparing of words she shortens it to 'coming tats'. To make the usage even more confusing, 'I'll have to be going, where's my ta-ta?' means: 'I'm off, where's my hat?' A weak-willed thesis writer confronted with this is likely to say 'ta ta' and go straight home to mother. If he remains he may learn that toffs are 'posh gits up west who we wouldn't give house room to'; but 'a toff', singular, is a fine fellow and a thorough gentleman.

Statements are contradictory, too. 'Ain't it all right, eh?' means it is far from all right; likewise 'isn't it bloody good?' and 'isn't it fair?' When a girl says 'Here comes the man I left home for' she is talking about a man she would not leave home for in any circumstances. If one asks why, the answer is 'Y's a crooked letter'. Cockneys are not concerned with why or when; they speak the Queen's English, and that is good enough. I once asked my father why cats were called 'sooners'. 'Sooner shit than eat', the old man replied. (Oh well, curiosity killed the cat.) Anyone who says 'I thought —' is inviting the response: 'You know what thought did.'

'I gave him a real right coating' has nothing to do with handing anyone a jacket; it means I gave him the length of my tongue ('Tisn't half a length, too' murmured my father apropos my mother). 'I didn't half pay him' is not about settling accounts but is another way of saying that he received a domino, or a right doughboy, or: I clocked him. 'I told him his fortune', usually said by women, is another misleading expression; it stands for a good telling-off.

The 'why' and the origins of these expressions are less important than the tone of voice in using them, because any one of them may have several meanings. 'Who's he when he's out?' usually conveys 'Never heard of him'. It can also mean 'That's a funny name' or 'a hell of a name to go to bed with'; on other occasions, 'Who does he think he is?' Strongly derogatory terms can also be affectionate ones. A perisher can be a swine but 'Hallo, you old perisher' and 'What's the little perisher up to?' are warmly friendly. Even 'tea leaf' can be used amiably. It depends how it is said. A native walks blindfold through this minefield, but the studious outsider all too often comes to grief.

William Matthews in his *Cockney Past and Present* showed that Cockney is a language in its own right, and worked hard to do it justice. Understanding (and useful) as his book is, it appears to accept literary renderings of Cockney that are simply abysmal — indeed, if they were less bad Matthews's plea would not have been so necessary. Decent, sympathetic semblances are rare; nevertheless, it is hard to swallow Matthews's commendation of Barry Pain's 'De Omnibus' as a good example of Cockney dialect. Allowing for the lapse of time, Pain's version is a distasteful parody.

I don't unnerstand Femiles. The other dye I 'appened ter pick up an extry 'Alf thick 'un throo puttin' money on my opinyun of the gran' neshnal. Well, nar, the fancy tikin' me, I drops in on a plice as were a cut above whart I patternized as a yooshal thing. As I sye, I were a-going to enjy myself, so I orders my steak, cut thick, underdone, an' my pint of Burton, sime as if I'd bin the Lord Meer isself. Then I tikes a look rarnd. Theer were two femiles as 'ed jest done. They were settin' doin' nothink. Theer were a witer oppersite ter them, close enough ter 'ave bit 'em, an' 'e weren't doin' nutthink neither. Pressintly a Gint calls in an' orf 'e goes.

The resemblance between this and Cockney speech is negligible. A key to Pain's attitude is 'throo'. Is there any other way of pronouncing 'through'? Of course not; but since he is writing-up a Cockney, he uses the phonetic spelling to squeeze an extra superior smile out of his readers. The same is true of 'opinyun' — it is the normal pronunciation, but without the spelling changed it would not look illiterate enough. Yet Pain misses authentic things which would suit the picture he is trying to give: 'me' for 'my' and 'gointer' for 'going to', and he obviously does not know whether or not to sustain the present tense. Here is the same passage in 20th-century Cockney.

Women are a licker to me. The other day, I picked up a quick half-bar through backing a good thing in the National. It skated home, and when I collared me winnings I went off for a good blow-out. Being well britched I wasn't going to no coffee stall, so I hops into one of these posh caffs, all chandeliers and flunkeys in stiff dickeys. There were a couple of birds sitting there who'd just done golloping their grub down, and they'd been feeding their faces so much they could hardly move. Not a stone's throw from them there was a waiter standing there like a tit in a trance. He wasn't showing much sign of life, not till a customer hollered at him — and then he was off so fast you couldn't see his arse for dust.

Undoubtedly the Cockney accent, as well as expressions in vogue, has undergone changes since Victorian times. Barry Pain's work was published about the turn of the century. This means that any person in the nineteen-twenties and -thirties knew many people who had grown to maturity by that time; if he was growing up, he modelled his speech on theirs. On this basis it is possible to say positively that Pain's 'Cockney' was *not* authentic for the period. To take this further, somebody born in the early 'twenties had grandparents who were born perhaps in 1860 or thereabouts and can remember curiosities in the way they talked.

The differences were only minor ones. Victorian Cockney seems to have been rather thin and reedy in its sound, not quite as full-bodied as it became in the mid-20th century. The grand-parents said 'gardin' for garden, and 'year'oles' for earholes, and their version of 'chimney' was 'chimbly'. The men also said 'Yus' a litle more frequently than younger people did. But they certainly did not say 'femiles' when they wanted to sound scornful about the other sex — grandfather called them 'women', as did all other males. Anyone who wishes to hear the authentic tones of the Victorian Cockney should try to get hold of a record of Gus Elen singing 'If it wasn't for the houses in between'.

One mysterious aspect of Cockney past and present is the way certain names have been picked on. 'Liz' was a highly popular name in the past; the East End was full of Lizzies. At the same time, it was thought to be funny. 'Skinny Liz' was the standard nickname for a thin girl or woman, and 'Frowzy Liz' for an unkempt one. 'Lizzy Dripping' was a contemptuous nickname.

'Sam' was equated with a soft-minded person: 'you must think I'm a Sammy', or 'I'm a Sammy', or 'I'm not going to be a Sammy for you'. It may have come from the Yiddish 'schlemiel', a simpleton. In later years 'Charlie' has been used in the same way: 'a right Charlie' is a dunce, a silly ass. Since 'Charlies' is an old term for the female breasts, this may be another form of older people's 'great tit' for a ninny. Algernon, Cecil and Cuthbert were thought laughable, and Clarence and Marmaduke hilarious, because they were names which went with top hats and spats. However, apart from the popularity of Lizzie, there were plenty of Samuels and Charleses. Why these names should continue to be widely used, at the same time as they were terms of ridicule, is decidedly odd. Perhaps some researcher can explain.

CHAPTER 7

Personal Matters

Publicly and collectively, Cockneys are all for sentimentality. The songs they cherish most drip with it: 'Nellie Dean', 'My Old Dutch', 'Little Annie Rooney', 'If You Were the Only Girl in the World', 'Comrades' — people's faces as they sing these together in pubs and at parties are a study in warm feeling. It goes wider than personal relationships into an open-hearted general human sympathy. 'The Blind Boy', 'My Fiddle is My Sweetheart', 'Skylark', 'If Those Lips Could Only Speak' express tenderness towards all those who have misfortunes, even the rich.

These songs are said to be 'nice' because they bring out such feelings. In the heyday of the cinema, girls and women wept copiously at sad scenes in romantic films; one could look round in a cinema and see the handkerchiefs dabbing eyes and noses. Nobody minded admitting this, and girls would talk about how much they cried as proof of a film's excellence.

The music halls were full of sentimentality as well as comedy. The Casey's Court show ended with a sketch called 'The Bloomsbury Burglars', and this had a sequel called 'My Pal Jerry'. Nobbler and Jerry, the two burglars, tried to escape from Dartmoor and Jerry died from exposure on the moor. At the point when the warders arrived and found him dead, Nobbler took the centre of the stage, removed his convict's cap and raised his eyes heavenward, and said in a dramatic voice: 'Gorn before a better judge!' That was the cue for every man in the house to feel a lump in his throat.

This communal enjoyment of exaggerated feeling seems to be a balance or safety-valve. Cockneys are deeply inhibited over displaying emotion person to person. It is the opposite of middle- and upper-class behaviour, in which crowd sentimentality is usually out of order but couples call each other 'darling' publicly and are demonstrative. East Enders, married or courting, do not use endearments or show affection in front of other people. Often they scarcely show it or speak about it at all. The exchange of kisses between relatives, or couples who are old friends, when they meet and part are a mixture of cordiality and tradition; it does not follow that a husband and wife who do it would kiss each other.

A well-established couple may use 'luv' or 'mate' to each other — it has to be an everyday-sounding word, not anything 'silly'. Small children are petted and given lots of baby-talk, but as they grow older the demonstrativeness tails off quickly: the child is said to have 'got past' that kind of thing. The time when affection for a person can be expressed unreservedly is when he or she has died. 'In Memoriam' notices containing flowery verses are put in the local papers for the anniversaries, and regular visits made to spouses' and parents' graves; to ignore them is to show a want of feeling.

~ ~

At the bottom of all this is a conviction that the emotions are not to be trusted: for sure, they will get you into trouble. When middle-aged couples sing with gusto 'I love you, Nellie Dean' they are not remembering their courtship, for it was never like that. They are attributing to it the sentiments which can be let loose safely only now and in this way. During courtship, if a boy talks or acts demonstratively the girl assumes he is 'after something'. In marriage, her conditioning tells her that if she gave and accepted open expressions of affection the result would be more slavery and babies. The boy or young man feels that her emotions would, if he allowed it, make inroads on his masculinity. The most either is likely to say is that he or she 'thinks a lot' of the other one; and it is proved by conduct rather than declarations.

Cockneys are seldom inarticulate, however. When a fellow and a girl have a liking for each other, their talk consists largely of abrasive banter. With fences up against words from the heart, they test each other in this way. The twitting and ripostes are an enjoyment in themselves, but are also a means of assessing attitudes and forbearance. If one of the couple makes a gesture of obvious regard — say, gives the other a present — he or she is self-deprecating about it, so as not to appear to have made an emotional opening. Underneath, of course, each wonders how much the other one likes him or her.

A piece of dialogue can illustrate this. The couple are 'going about together'; imagine them sitting on one of the benches near Watney Street market.

Betsy: Thank Gawd for a sit down, my feet are killing me. I wish

	you wouldn't take me out on these walks.
Bill:	Me take you — I like that. You lug me all round the houses, get me to look at half the shops in Stepney — and when you feel tired, who gets the blame? Joe Soap!
Betsy:	Well, you wanted to take me out, and walking me round the shops was taking me out. Anyway, I'm sitting here for the next hour and I'm not moving; you want to do any more walking and you can do it on your Jack.
Bill:	I'm not sure who took who now, but I know one thing and that ain't two — I've seen enough furniture shops to last me a lifetime. I don't know what you women see in furniture, I don't straight.
Betsy:	That's enough about women. You men would look blue without us. You can't do a hand's turn for yourselves. You all want waiting on. Who changed your shitty napkins for you when you were a kid? I bet it wasn't your old man.
Bill:	Now she's going to start nagging me. That's all I'm short of.
Betsy:	Nagging's good for you, it keeps you alive. Nagging's what you need.
Bill:	I'm getting it whether I need it or not.
Betsy:	Ah, shurrup. I'm tired of arguing with you. All I want to do is sit here and have a quiet smoke.
Bill:	You'll choke yourself if you're not careful. How long have you been smoking anyway?
Betsy:	Couple of days. No use, I'll never get the hang of it. Here, you have the rest of the packet. Save throwing them away.
Bill:	Crafty bugger, ain't you?
Betsy:	Why?
Bill:	You know why.
Betsy:	All right, I bought you a few fags: what's wrong with that? You bought me enough things when you were working, so why can't I buy you something? And don't go slinging them back at me either.
Bill:	I ought to. If anyone else did it I'd spit in their eye. All right, I'll take them, sod you. All the same, don't do it again, will you?
Betsy:	No. Not till next time.
Bill:	You do and I'll murder you.
Betsy:	Now he's threatening me. I don't know why I put up with him, I don't straight. It ain't his looks — he might get by on a dark night, but that's about all — and it ain't his brains — he's

	a dozy ha'porth. And it ain't that either, so shut your row.
Bill:	I ain't saying a dicky bird.
Betsy:	No, but you're thinking it. I know you of old: you've got a dirty mind.

The usual advice to girls, once they start going about with boys, is 'Keep your hand on your ha'penny'. It is a telling piece of imagery, since they were warned in the same way when they first went to the shops for their mothers: if the ha'penny gets lost there won't be another to replace it. In general Cockneys have always had a high standard of sexual morality. The tradition came from hard economic necessity — an unmarried girl who 'got into trouble' had created a disaster for herself. Likewise, infidelity was disgraceful because it left dependents in the lurch. In these terms, not only was immorality an upper-class pastime but romance — sweet words to rouse the senses — was for those who could afford the consequences.

On top of these basic considerations, morality was dictated by shortage of opportunities. Few homes allowed privacy. On the outer fringe of the East End open spaces such as the Hackney and Leyton marshes, Beckton marshes and Epping Forest were available. The last was too far out to be much use, and the police kept an eye on the marshes at night. Girls who went to these places with males were considered loose, and harmed their chances of being taken up by other fellows. To the extent that couples went in for cuddling and feeling, it took place in the kitchen after the rest of the family had gone to bed or in the doorway on the excuse of 'saying goodnight' — circumstances where advanced sexual contact would quickly be found out (another place was the back seats in the cinema).

In addition, contraception was very difficult. The idea of devices for it was still new up to 1939. A good many older women, despite their sufferings through lack of it, thought it was unnatural and therefore wrong and passed this on to their daughters. To Catholics it was an abomination, of course. Only two methods were known among working people. One of them, 'Rendell's', was for female use; besides the fact that it was rather messy, there was a legend that in every packet of the things one had to be a dud by order of the government.

This left 'french letters'. Respectable chemists, including Boot's, did not sell them and would often tick off a young man who asked for them: that was still the case some time after 1945. Obtaining them was a hole-and-corner business, so embarrassing as to be a deterrent in itself to those who were thinking of anticipating marriage — fellows bought razor-blades instead if the shop had a girl assistant, if other customers came in, or if their nerve failed them. Married men made their purchases in barbers' shops, often without saying a word: a coin held up, a meaning twitch of the eyebrows, and a quick exchange between palms.

Thus, most East Enders of both sexes were virgins when they married. Those who managed not to be got their experience, if not on the marshes, 'against the wall'. This was intercourse standing up in a doorway or some other secluded spot, and it was called 'a knee-trembler'. However, it was boasted about much more than it was actually done. For masculine reputation's sake a lot of young men liked to convey that they were well-seasoned sexually, but the phrases used were (and are still) rather nebulous: 'getting something', 'having a bit', or 'some of the other'. The last is extracted from 'this, that and the other' and means 'you know what I mean'; it is used to make almost any contact with a girl sound orgiastic.

Better incomes, the spread of knowledge and availability of contraception, and the motor-car, have altered the scene in the last twenty years. Probably the majority now have sex before marriage, but it is still tied to fairly stringent ideas of family life. Girls allow it because fellows want it and privacy and safety are possible, but there has to be an understanding that the couple will marry anyway. And a sizeable number stick to the convention of no sex before marriage. The Cockney boy thinks highly of this, and is gratified when his girl is adamant about it even though he keeps on trying. Some practise a double standard, hunting sexual scalps but wanting to marry virgins; others believe seriously that they themselves should wait until they are married. Sex remains largely a condition in an economic bargain, and the hard-boiled nature of courtship conversations demonstrates this.

~ ~

Male Cockneys speak about sex a great deal among themselves. It is seldom direct, explicit talk but is mostly on the themes of virility and the unknowability of women. Boys are brought up to the idea of being masculine. They learn that males do not cry and must be self-assertive, and as they grow older each one must represent himself as an implacable fellow sexually. Even aged men talk like this; they want to be seen noticing women and to advertize that they are still keen on a bit.

The 'obscene' words are used comparatively little in sexual talk. Despite their commonness for emphasizing, name-calling, and colouring-up everyday speech, most men shy away from applying them as they are meant; to do so is ultra-coarse. The word for sex is 'it', with a wide range of meanings. 'It' is sexuality in general as well as the sex act specifically. Young men will say of a girl 'Do you fancy it?' = would you like to have sex with her? 'At it' means having intercourse. Of a dopey or effeminate person they say 'he wouldn't know what to do with it if he got it': he looks as if he would be useless sexually. 'It' is also the male private parts, or the female ones. In any of these senses the word is used and comprehended by everyone; pub comedians raise their cheapest and loudest laughs by throwing it about.

I heard several East Enders' opinions on sexual language at the time of the *Lady Chatterley's Lover* trial in 1960. All said that, familiar as they were with the words, they could not conceive a man using them to a woman as Mellors does in the book. A middle-aged woman told me emphatically: 'I might say to my husband "That was a nice bunk-up we had last night" — but I'd never say *those* words, nor would he.' To many working people the shockingness was not simply in the words but in the idea of their being used by a man of low social status to a lady. On the other hand, it is understood that at higher social levels talk and conduct are lax compared with Cockneys' own. That does not make things all right; on the contrary, it reinforces the belief that 'superior' people are nothing of the kind and should be kept at arm's length.

Women's feelings about sex, and how they talk about it, are a mystery to most men. They assume that women like it less than men, that it is something males seek compulsively and women grant or with-hold according to their moods. Cockney women do not do much to alter these beliefs, and (perhaps with justification) treat sex as a battlefield in which they must hold their ground at all costs. Characteristically, married men say (I quote an old friend) 'It's all right at first till the novelty wears off for them, then all you get is "Gawd, aren't you bleedin' heavy!"'

The need for sex is acknowledged as 'nature', but no self-respecting woman would ask her husband for it or make known that she enjoys it as men do. I have heard women talking about Jewesses they worked with, who did not have that inhibition; it was seen as proof that Jews were different from gentiles — more hot-blooded. Very many women never let their husbands see them undressed. Probably this is partly a reaction to a shortage of privacy, but it is also keeping men in their place sexually.

Girls are taken into their mothers' confidence and conditioned over these matters, and the clanning-together heightens men's conviction that women have sexual secrets. A surprising number of men leave contraception to their wives without saying anything, thinking that they can deal with what happens to their bodies. Married women are supposed to become progressively more knowing about such things and to be able to dispose of unwanted pregnancies (the legendary cure is gin and Beecham's Pills). A lot of unmarried girls also believe this about older women, and if they find themselves 'in trouble' will seek out some mature friend or relative in hopes that she can tell them what to do.

To be pregnant is to be 'expecting', 'carrying' or 'in the family way', have 'a bun in the oven', or be 'in the club'. The last is short for 'in the pudden club', and developed from an earlier saying that someone conspicuously pregnant looked as if she had been eating bread pudding; the 'club' idea arose from gatherings of expectant mothers at clinics and hospitals. A woman who thinks she is pregnant explains that she has 'seen nothing', i.e. has missed her periods, or simply 'I haven't seen'. When she has had what seems a sufficient number of children, other women are sure to say to her: 'Going to shut up shop now?'

From women's point of view, sex is closely associated with all kinds of burdens for them while men know only the pleasure-giving side of it. Nevertheless, they would not be East Enders if they did not enjoy talk and quite a lot of vulgarity among themselves. Between the sexes, they know exactly the balance between what is and what is not permitted. For instance, go to any greengrocer's stall where men are serving cucumbers and tomatoes to women, for an earful of ripe allusions; but it is amusement for a female audience, and would be unacceptable if other men were there. One Saturday while this book was being written, my wife stood near two women at a shop window in Whitechapel. They gazed at a pottery model of some lemons, and one said: 'They look like your tits.' 'Blimey', said the other, 'I can't take you anywhere.' They both laughed, but the second one had made her point: *not* in front of a lady we don't know.

~ ~

A relationship which has always been specially important to Cockneys is 'mates'. It comes next to family, and like family it provides feelings of security. The word 'friend' does not fully cover it. Friends are the people he knows and likes, but 'mates' means exclusive closeness and mutual support.

Everyone is expected to have a mate. 'We've been mates for years' is often stressed: the relationship is a lasting one. Girls usually speak of 'my mate' before they are married, when the person becomes 'my friend', but the term continues lifelong among men. Other words for mate are the rhyming 'china' (i.e. 'china plate') and 'oppo', short for 'opposite number' — an expression learnt in the services.

The closeness normally starts in the early teens. Mates seldom have real quarrels. If a break does take place there is a deep sense of loss on both sides; in most cases both parties would like to find a way to patch things up, however bitter the row has been. A music-hall song expresses the feeling:

> For old times' sake, don't let this enmity live —
> For old times' sake, let us forget and forgive.
> Life's too short for sorrow, hearts are too precious to break:
> Shake hands and let us be friends, for old times' sake.

Steadfastness is taken for granted. The mate must be on hand in times of material or psychological need. Not only the two concerned but all who know of the relationship expect that. If a young man has troubles, his mother or father may say: 'Where's your mate, then — I thought he was supposed to help you? Fine mate he is!' Often the mate is hardly any better placed, and any help he can offer is a long way from substantial; but his willingness is what counts. In wartime mates decided which of the services they would join together, and when one takes up with a girl it is essential for the other one to approve.

Next to *the* mate come 'mates', the crowd one knocks about with. Each of them has his or her own particular mate. From the time of these affiliations few fresh friends are made. If one of the crowd does so, he may feel a little guilty. When the newcomer is introduced, he understands that he may have to take a back seat for a time: old mates come first. If these groups are dispersed by marriage and changes, the Cockney's need for a circle of allies and intimates remains; and having once been a mate means a permanent bond.

'Chum' has never been a working-class word. It is used in a special way by Cockneys to address someone who is presuming. 'Yes, chum?' stands for 'What are you doing here, and who are you anyway?' Likewise 'Watch it, chum!' advises the person that he has no standing and is asking for trouble. When this warning note is not being sounded the word still implies an alien presence. 'My old chum here' means 'this fellow whom I know nothing about'. It is possible that the term was taken up deliberately as a social class backhander, to express a difference in assumptions about relationships.

Friendship at every stage of life is valued very highly by Cockneys. The sight of women, particularly older ones, talking together often produces a chorus of

> Dear old pals, jolly old pals,
> Always together in all sorts of weather.
> Dear old pals, faithful old pals —
> Give me the friendship of dear old pals!

But the singing is never derogatory. It means what it says, that their matiness is lovely to behold; the singers hope that they themselves will always have such cronies.

It is expected that neighbours know one another's business and be in one another's confidence. Until recent years housing made this more or less inevitable, and the strongest of all complaints against blocks of flats is that they have destroyed neighbourliness. The degrees of intimacy reflected physical closeness, and this was — and, from long-standing habit, is still — stated when persons were mentioned. Cockneys have seldom ever said 'neighbour' by itself. It is 'my next-door neighbour' or 'my next-door-but-one', or 'she lives just opposite' or 'three doors away from me'; it may even be 'my neighbour over the back' or 'a few doors up on the other side'. The phrases convey places in the scale of relationships as accurately as 'brother-in-law', 'second cousin' etc. within a family.

~ ~

There is no Cockney word for homosexuality; it was virtually unknown before being publicized in recent years. 'Queer' has always meant 'ill', and older East Londoners still use it in that sense — 'I've heard that Fred is very queer'. It is also used in the phrase 'the queer fellow': the person everyone talks about, you know who I mean. Up to 1939 'nancy-boy' and 'pansy' were names for elegantly-dressed young men. During military service in the war (or if they went to prison) men came across homosexuality and a new meaning for 'nancy-boy', but it remained a distant abnormality. Today 'poof' is used, and Cockneys have a rhyming slang version of it: 'horse's hoof'. There is also a reminder of the former meaning in the term 'ponced-up' for over-dressed and -groomed.

Though 'bugger' is probably the commonest of all swear-words among Cockneys (women use it as well as men), the majority are unaware of its meaning. If they are told it, they regard it as too specialized to affect their everyday usage. The traditional sex-roles have still a strong hold in East London, and the existence of anything else among them is more or less inconceivable to most people. In the late 'thirties and 'forties a small group of men with high-heeled shoes and rouged faces appeared late at nights at coffee stalls in Clapton and Leyton. They were thought a curiosity; if they were mentioned in conversation someone might say 'My aunt's read all about them, and she says they can't help being like that!'

This does not mean that Cockneys are tolerant of sexual un-orthodoxies. They are not; the absence of terms for them stands for a

lack of recognition or comprehension. The only ones which are found
amusing are (a) the alleged connection between sailors and sodomy,
and (b) 'flashers'. The first is a joke because no-one really believes it; in
the second, the idea of a man exposing himself to shock women has
comic possibilities which cannot be ignored. 'Flasher' is actually a
word devised by the police — the original expression was 'flashing his
Hampton' (Hampton Wick: rhyming slang). Otherwise, the Cockney
sees them as attacks on the manhood and womanhood he is used to, and
usually he (or she) is strongly antagonistic towards them.

Prostitution also gets little or no recognition in East End language,
yet it was rife throughout the 19th century and persisted up to recent
years. The reason is that it never touched everyday life; it belonged to
the seamen and on-the-move immigrants. These were numerous
enough, gathering in pubs in Limehouse and Stepney (in the years after
the last war, before re-building, it was cafes in Cable Street). However,
families grew up and went about their affairs without ever seeing a
prostitute and knowing only by hearsay that the trade existed. The
greater number of the girls and women came from outside, drawn to the
docks as others found their customers at main-line stations.

A good many were drawn also by the proliferation of charities in East
London. As an area desperate with overcrowding, homelessness and
every kind of social problem, it was a magnet to societies for doing good
in the 19th century. Thus, it offered the prostitute or the intending one
not only opportunities but some hope of help if times grew bad. Today
the position of the celebrated meths drinkers is the same. The majority
are not wayward East Enders but Scots and Irishmen; they come to
'Itchy Park' — Spitalfields churchyard — because of the shelter and the
charitable interest in them there. Notable as they may be, they are not
part of Cockney life, and there is no term or nickname for them. The
words used for prostitution are the ugly commonplace ones. Very
occasionally 'brass', short for the fairground 'brassnail', can be heard.
'Ponce' has been a term of abuse for fifty years; it means an unpleasant
parasite, and is used as a verb to the same effect — 'he was poncing on
the old man'.

~ ~

A prostitute is not called a tart by Cockneys, because 'tart' has always
meant a girl. It is a street word, not used indoors, but it is not coarse or
unpleasant. It conveys a well made up, attractive girl. One might say
'Who's that ginger-haired tart,' or 'Harry was talking to a tart', or even
'your tart' — though the last shows a poor vocabulary and would be said
only by children. The term has been going strong for at least seventy

years, and probably derives from something like 'jam tart'; given that, why should a reference to colourfulness and sweetness be offensive?

In the 'thirties 'dame' was borrowed from American films. Since the war 'bird' has been used in the same way as 'tart'. It was middle-class slang in the 'thirties; its extensive use probably came from the radio, where 'tart' would have been avoided because of its non-Cockney meaning. 'Bride' had a few years' run but was not widely popular; it meant a sexually willing girl — 'Let's see if we can pick up a couple of brides'. At the present time young East Enders are using 'a richard' for a girl. This was devised by teddy boys in the mid-fifties, 'Richard the Third' to rhyme with 'bird'.

The other common expression is 'a bit'. It may be filled out according to the speaker's frame of mind. Older women will talk about a young one as 'a bit of stuff' or 'a bit of skirt' (the latter is play on the name of a cheap cut of meat from the butcher); men say 'a bit of the other' or 'a bit of crumpet'. In common everyday use: 'that's a nice-looking bit', 'I saw you with a bit', 'those two bits over there', etc. Ultimately the term is rather contemptuous, only a little less depersonalizing than the American 'a piece of ass'.

Of course all this is sexist, but most Cockneys would deny that women are subservient to men in practice. The widespread idea of the mature Cockney woman seems to be akin to George Orwell's pen-pictures of the proles in *Nineteen Eighty-Four:* 'Two bloated women, one of them with her hair coming down'; 'Two monstrous women with brick-red forearms folded across their aprons were talking outside a doorway'; 'a monstrous woman, solid as a Norman pillar, with brawny red forearms and a sacking apron strapped about her middle . . . Whenever her mouth was not corked with clothes pegs she was singing in a powerful contralto.'

As a corrective to this sort of thing, it is useful to remember that the word Cockney is supposed to mean a weakling or undersized person: Middle English 'coken-ey', a cock's egg. Though they come in all shapes and sizes, Cockneys are not characteristically big people. The great East End boxers were predominantly light-weights, nine-and-a-half-stone men. If a 'typical' Cockney woman had to be shown, she would be on the small side. By tradition they rule their homes and their husbands, and are tougher than men.

In hard times they needed to be. Men worked long hours for meagre wages; their wives worked even longer to raise families and keep heads above water. It was the women who produced meals out of thin air, stalled the debt-collectors and wheedled a little extra out of the pawnbrokers. The burden of bad housing fell chiefly on them: they coped with overcrowding and toiled to keep slum houses clean, and often went out charring as well to help the family finances. The struggle made them unsentimental, and they were known for caustic tongues. Almost any woman could drive her husband out of the house by nagging, but could also say to one of the children when cash was short: 'Take this money and get your father a packet of Woodbines, a man can't go without a smoke.'

The man was nominally the head of the household. As bread-winner he was privileged to raise cain if his tea was not ready and waiting when he came home from work, and to object if the food was not to his liking. Very few men helped in the home. Washing-up and cleaning were women's work, and a man who did such things was scorned for being under his wife's thumb: 'she leads him by the nose', or 'she wears the trousers in that house'.

Women shared these assumptions and made those remarks, and they did not want their husbands to be butts for others' jokes. Thus, if (in a rare moment of weakness) a man offered to help, the wife was bound to say: 'You keep out from under my feet, you're more trouble than you're worth.' It did not stop her complaining that he was bone-idle when women's work was never done, but neither of them thought the contradiction answerable within the framework of custom.

Men were expected to take their wives out on Saturday or Sunday evenings, and over this the woman had all the say. The outing might be to a pub or a variety theatre, or to visit a relative, or to sit in the park if the weather was fine. The wife insisted on her husband's being respectably turned out: 'Smarten yourself up! I'm not going out with you dressed any old how!' If they went visiting the talk consisted largely of gossip about neighbours and friends; they cracked jokes and laughed a lot, and went home reasonably content.

The convention which men imposed unrelentingly on women was hostility to the idea of wives going to work. Charring did not really count, since it was casual employment for an hour or two at a time, but that was still disliked. Letting the wife go out to a job was thought unmanly — it implied that the husband was failing to support her. Many men caused needless hardship to their families by their intransigence on this point. When numerous married women went to work in the post-war years, the voice of tradition still threw all the responsibility on the husbands; it was said that men were 'sending' their wives, or 'making them go', to work.

Since they have been able to lay down this kind of economic yea-and-nay, men must be seen as the Cockney dominant sex. In other respects their authoritarianism was more ritual than reality in the past; women worked from morning to night in the home, and ordered everyone and everything in it. Today the pattern is changing as the result of fewer children, less drudgery — less of everything which made Shaw in 1912 and Orwell in 1947 agree that working-class women were old in their thirties — and the general spread of ideas. The change starts in courtship. Formerly the young man's paying for his girl wherever they went was a token that he would be a good provider, but more sharing is expected now. Couples know that their standard of living depends on both of them having jobs and making domestic arrangements accordingly. Nevertheless, they have learned roles and habits from the older generations; and these are probably still the strongest force in their relationships inside the home.

~ ~

Cockneys' greatest fear is of illness. It has several causes. The fear of loss of income; a woman's conviction that her family will not survive if she is not there to do everything for them; general dread of medical treatment and hospitals.

On those accounts, considerable degrees of discomfort and illness are often endured rather than going to the doctor. In the past, people professed to know what was wrong with them, and to be able to deal with it themselves. Part of a wife's duties was to treat her husband's and her children's ailments: hot flannel for internal pains, camphor rub for the chest, poultices, 'drawing ointments', as well as laxatives and emetics. A lot of conversation among women was about these things, the exchange of advice and experiences.

Those who went to doctors with their ailments knew, likewise, what they were going to get. There seemed to be two prescriptions which covered everything. One of them was ipecacuanha mixture; as scribbled on the slip to take to the chemist's the words looked like 'Mystic Spec', and the medicine was known and even asked for by this name. For most people the doctor's was the ultimate resort. Women, conscious that they would carry the burden of any illness in their families, preached prevention: wrap up warmly, avoid draughts and damp. Damp in particular was held to cause colds, rheumatism and piles, and to be involved in more serious illnesses.

Phrases for being in poor health have not altered. 'None too rosy', 'a bit weak on one's pins', 'not up to the mark', 'a bit dicky' (probably from 'Uncle Dick', sick). 'A touch of the inky blue' means flu; rheumatism, sciatica, fibrositis etc. are called 'the screws'. With the same characteristic understatement, a person with bronchial troubles who coughs unceasingly is described, and describes himself, as 'chesty'. Pneumonia is 'pew-' or 'phew-monia', another malapropism devised to broaden the meaning (up to the middle 'forties it was usually a killing illness).

A person in hospital is 'in dock', an obvious metaphor in East London. 'Laid up' is another shipping expression; it means ill in bed at home. If the hospital patient is dangerously ill, he or she is 'on the gate'. This refers to pre-war arrangements, when visits and enquiries outside a twice-a-week routine were allowed only for critical cases and the gatekeeper had a list of them. 'On the special' was another term for the same thing.

The old feeling about hospitals, which still lingers, is that one might go in and not come out. Elderly people voice it today: 'I keep getting a sore throat but I'm afraid to tell the doctor, he may want to send me to hospital' was heard from an old lady recently. 'I'm not going to go there and let them cut me about', or 'Who wants to be messed about by students?' used to express the belief that hospitals experimented on the poor for the benefit of the rich. In the 'thirties there was a persistent story that Bart's Hospital was willing to buy anyone's body for use after his death. Another story, which may well have been true, was that women who had to be taken to hospital after illegal abortions were deliberately given a rough time.

Many patients were in a hopeless condition when they went into hospital. Working men with internal troubles could not afford diets or staying at home; sick pay — 'Panel money' — was not enough to live on, and plenty of bosses would fire men who had time off through illness. By the time they saw a doctor and were put in dock, their state was dire. Certain general hospitals had the reputation of being 'dying hospitals'; in the circumstances it was hardly fair.

Individual doctors have always been highly respected in the East End, and anyone who works at the London Hospital in Whitechapel today gets 'served well' by the local stallholders. The 'Panel' doctor in the past was often like a village doctor who knew and sympathized with local problems. He would try to squeeze extra vouchers for milk and eggs for unemployed people from the RO and make unpaid off-duty visits, and was known as 'a toff' and 'a real gentleman'. Doctors and patients alike knew that poverty and malnutrition were their greatest enemy, disguised in phrases like 'nervous debility' and 'run down'.

'Time' is used specially to mean childbirth. Deriving from the common advance-notice sense ('her time's not due for a month yet'), it has become the word for labour. Women say 'I remember my time', or 'I had a bad time with my Susan'. The expression for lying-in is 'gone to bed with another baby' — 'to have' instead of 'with' would be too descriptive. In the same vein of avoiding to-the-point words in this mattter, a midwife is rarely called that and is almost always 'the nurse'.

The most common term for dying is the formal 'pass away'. Slang terms for it have never been uttered easily, and jocularities such as 'pushing up the daisies' for someone dead are in bad taste. 'On the last knockings' or 'hasn't got long to go' are for a fatal illness. 'He rolled up' or 'he pegged out' mean a person has died, but both refer to burial — rolled in a blanket, and the site of the grave pegged out. One other expression is 'his arse is cold'. It can be compared with the present-day Americanism 'get my [your, his] ass out of here' meaning to remove oneself. In both, 'arse' is used for the entire body or carcass. 'Put one's head in the gas oven' means commit suicide, because that was the normal method for most of this century; and the phrase is still used, even by people who live in all-electric flats.

CHAPTER 8

Moods and Circumstances

The Cockney would feel a failure if he were short of apt words for any occasion. If there is no occasion he is likely to produce a phrase or comment by way of 'making conversation'. Parodied philosophical remarks serve this purpose. 'Well, if things don't alter they'll stay as they are'; 'Such is life without a wife' — these are silence- or ice-breakers (the response to the second is 'and it's a bloody sight worse when you've got one').

For an anti-climax or a disappointment there is 'After the Lord Mayor's show comes the dust cart', or 'What you gain on the swings you lose on the roundabouts', or 'Oh well, there's another day tomorrow'. The standard mock-rueful observation is 'Dear mother, it's a bastard'. This is supposed to be an Army recruit's letter home; the next person should answer 'Dear son, so are you', and the first speaker completes the dialogue with 'Dear mother, sell the donkey and buy me out'.

Explanations of how things work or have come about are usually capped with 'And that's how the milk got in the coconut!' or 'Now you know how many beans make five'. The latter is not at all meaningless. Every Cockney child is asked that question and learns the answer: 'Six if you're a buyer, four if you're a seller'. For those who persist in asking 'the answer's a lemon', which leads to 'suck it and see'.

Cockneys are sceptics, so statements of alleged facts and accounts of personal experience have to be accompanied by special assurances that they are true. Children have recognized ways of swearing the truth of something: 'God's honour!'; wetting the forefinger with spittle, holding it up and reciting 'See this wet, see this dry, cut my throat if I tell a lie'. If doubts are still expressed, 'On my mother's life!' can squash them: fathers and sisters are expendable, but mothers are sacred.

Adults' assurances are 'I saw it with my own eyes', 'it's as true as I'm standing here', 'as God is my witness' (or 'as God is my judge'), 'I'll swear it on a stack of bibles'. For extra impressiveness: 'May I never walk out of this room alive', or 'may I never see my wife and children alive again if this ain't true'. A story without these guarantees — for example, one which begins 'A lot of people wouldn't credit this, but I know you'll believe it' — should always be treated with reserve. 'If you don't believe me ask anyone, they'll tell you' is another weak assurance. A person averring that he would not be persuaded to do something by anyone says: 'Not for King Dick I wouldn't!'.

The hearer who is having none of what he is told replies 'I'll believe it when I see it'. If the story is altogether too tall, the response — particularly in a group — is to sing 'And the band played "Believe it if you like"!' Indignant disbelief takes the form of 'May you be forgiven for telling such lies'. When the story is a leg-pull, the teller may make his position clear with: 'It's as true as I'm riding this bicycle.'

There is a wide selection of expressions for a person who can never be believed. To mislead or misinform is to 'kid' or 'kid up'; hence he is a 'kidder' or 'a bit of a kidpot, on the quiet'. ('On the quiet' makes the description of the fellow's habits confidential; it is the Cockney version of 'between ourselves'.) He 'tells more lies than a horse can gallop', or 'can't half tell you the tale of the old iron pot' (i.e. play on the emotions), or 'if ever he told the truth the skies would fall'. Alternatively, you 'can't believe a blind word he says'. 'Blind' is widely used as in 'blinding', as a substitute for stronger adjectives; here, it implies that the man's words cannot be trusted even when he swears to them.

'Chancer' has come to mean a liar, but up to the last twenty years or so it was less definite and meant someone of doubtful credibility. He 'chanced it' or 'chanced his arm' when he spoke: that is, he gambled on not being found out. The hearer also took a chance if he believed him. 'Twicer' stands for a deceitful person — he has two stories, is two-faced, etc.; but the word is used also because it is close to 'twister'.

The smooth talker is not quite the same thing. He 'tells the tale' or 'can't half spin you a fanny'. A specialist in tall stories is a 'sprucer', and East Enders also speak of 'schmoozers'. A schmoozer's stock-in-trade is blarney, mainly designed to get round girls. Someone with a reputation for making and breaking promises is 'always going to shit miracles, till the time comes'; and 'with him it's a case of wish in one hand, shit in the other'. Empty talk is 'guiver'. A person who is full of it has 'too much of what the cat licks its arse with'.

~ ~

Contempt brings out the most colourful of Cockney speech. 'He's a nice bloke — nobody likes him' and 'he's a good fellow — to himself' are heavy condemnations. 'The more I see of him the less I like him', 'I can't a-bear him', 'can't stomach him', 'wouldn't give him houseroom' (or 'wouldn't give him the time of day') mean what they say. They can be expanded into 'I wouldn't talk to him if he was the last one on earth', and 'wouldn't touch him with a ten-foot barge-pole'.

More is said about friends whose conduct has been unworthy. 'If he comes round here any more I'll slam the door in his face'; 'I wouldn't talk to him if he went down on his hands and knees'; 'he'd cut your throat for twopence' and 'he'd swear your life away'; 'she looks as if butter wouldn't melt in her mouth, the two-faced bitch'; 'she wouldn't have the guts to say it to your face, the backbiting bleeder'. The person has spoiled things where he was once a favourite: 'he's shit in his nest'.

Derogatory remarks are for people who are not loved, but they do not carry strong personal feeling; they are for foremen, rent-collectors, Labour Exchange clerks and so on. 'Look at old Creeping Jesus', or 'here comes Ballocky Bill'; 'he's all right till the doctor sees him'; 'your mother may love you but you're a pain in the arse to me'. A standard piece of depreciation is 'Some say "Good old Charlie" — others speak the truth'. If it is behind Charlie's back, the 'others' ending may be varied by as many people as are present; the politest version is 'others reserve their opinion'.

Women have their own repertoire of scornful comments on men. 'I wouldn't go out with him, I'd sooner be shot than poisoned'; 'I wouldn't have him, not if his arse hung in diamonds'; 'I've seen better things than him crawl out of cheese'. 'Give it to the girl next door' is a rejection of a man's sexual advances — it comes from a song:

> I don't want it, I told you so before,
> Take it away, take it away,
> Give it to the girl next door.

In the same vein, amorous approaches are rebuffed with: 'You fancy yourself, don't you?' or the sarcastic 'Oh yes, I'm full of those tricks' (a variant of the latter is 'I'm full of tricks, but that's not one of them'). To the fellow who says 'Come out with me and I'll give you the time of your life' the stock answer is 'No thanks, I'm right off luxuries'.

Saturnine or gloomy-looking people are disliked by Cockneys; they identify this sort of demeanour with an uncharitable nature. Often the person is dubbed 'Smiler' or 'Laughing Boy'. (Ironic nicknames are fairly common. I have known a tiny underdeveloped man called 'Muscles' and a boss who never dropped anyone a penny called 'Tippo'.) He may also be called 'misery-guts', as others for equivalent reasons are 'greedy-guts', 'fat-guts', 'grizzle-guts' (i.e. a lachrymose female) etc.

Otherwise the gloomy person has got a face 'like a wet week' or 'as long as Mile End Road', or 'a face like a kite'. He 'would be the life and soul of any funeral', sitting there 'like a ray of sunshine'. If he is thin, he is 'a streak' — or 'a rasher' — 'of misery'. If he is well-off, they say 'Look at him: money and misery!'

That is not to say Cockneys cannot be melancholy. On the contrary, a Cockney with 'the hump' can be truly eloquent. 'Not a soul's been nigh nor by for weeks'; 'I haven't got a soul in the whole wide world'; 'haven't a thing to call my own'; 'no-one to get me a ha'porth of anything'; 'nobody cares if I live or die'; 'I've got no-one to turn to' or 'not a soul to talk to'; it'd fair break your heart if you was to see her now'.

~ ~

A slow or absent-minded person is addressed as 'Dreamy Daniel' or 'Come on, lightning!' He is 'a dozy ha'porth' and 'too slow to catch a cold', and 'not quick on the uptake'. More crudely, he can be called 'bacon-bonce' or 'pudden-headed' and told: 'shift your bloody self!' A more good-natured admonition to hurry is 'Come on, hop about!' If he is inept, a habitual muddler, he is like ' a wet nellie' or 'a fairy on a rock cake' or 'a Drury Lane fairy' or 'a Japanese whatsit'. 'You're a lively bloke, you are' may be for slowness, but is also said about a silly or thoughtless action.

The cruelty of some of these expressions reflects the struggle for existence. Cockneys have their share, and probably more, of kindliness; but it is important to them that every man should hold his own or he will drag others behind with him. Some sorts of disability and suffering — blindness most of all — cannot be pitied and helped enough, but others get little compassion.

Bad eyesight and deafness are mildly ridiculed: 'boss-eye', 'cock-eyed', 'silly old sod can't hear a bleeding word you say to him', as well as 'four-eyes' and 'Mutt and Jeff'. Terms for mental troubles show even greater insensitivity. 'Loony', 'barmy', 'not all there', 'crackers', 'up the pole', 'meshuga', 'got a screw loose', 'batty', 'loopy', 'doolally tap', 'off his onion', 'off his rocker', 'Lakes of Killarney'; any of these is supplemented by tapping the side of the head with the index finger. The person spoken about 'ought to be in Colney Hatch' or 'in Claybury' (those being mental hospitals for East London; before the last war Brentwood was another). Since the war 'round the bend', 'round the twist', and 'a nut case' or 'a nutter' have been added.

These terms are used as banter, of course. 'You're barmy' or 'he's off his rocker' are thrown about as good-humoured derision; they may contain admiration for someone's daring or his whimsicality. Nevertheless, they are the words and phrases for the unstable and defective. Though most Cockneys today would agree that mental troubles are illnesses, the feeling is still that decent people do not get them. 'He's crackers' means not so much 'he has become ill' as 'he is not, and has never been, one of us'. There is room for a lot of enlightenment — if it were not such a luxury in the East End.

Waste of money also produces hard words. Anyone who spends extravagantly 'has got more money than sense' or 'must like chucking it about'. 'If I had his money I'd know what to do with it' means either that the person is cautious beyond reason or that he is a spendthrift; one way or the other, a wrong sense of values. If it is a friend or one of the family, the comments are 'Can't you find anything better to do with your money?' and 'You paid how much for that? They must have seen you coming!' (There is also a bit of irony for when a 'careful' person unexpectedly puts his hand in his pocket for a small amount: 'Throwing your money about like a man with no arms.')

This is the chief criticism of excessive drinkers. The single man who has one over the eight, and anyone who gets merry at a party, are all right (as long as they don't get stroppy or become nuisances); but a habitually boozy married man is judged severely. He is 'a piss-tank' — more explicitly, 'he pisses his money up against the wall' and 'it would be more to his credit if he spent it on his wife and kids instead of giving it to the publican'.

Cockneys' distaste for wastefulness and their abhorrence of meanness are different sides of the same attitude. It is not decent to with-hold from one's dependents anything one is capable of giving. The necessities of life have an absolute priority, and after them should come treats and comforts. A lot maintain that the place for any surplus money is 'on your back', i.e. spend it on clothing. The majority of Cockneys have never been savers but praise the idea of providing for a rainy day — having 'a little bit put by' or 'something to fall back on'. The factors which usually prevent it being realized are the strong fear of being thought stingy, and the tradition in favour of snapping up satisfactions in case the chance does not recur. To say that somebody is 'not short of a couple of bob' or has got 'something under the floorboards' (or 'tucked under the mattress') conveys a slightly grudging admiration; it may be the same person who 'wouldn't give you the smell of an oil-rag', or 'all he'll give you is the itch'.

Expenditure is always a serious matter. Cockneys say 'out of debt, out of danger' when settling-up: as a self-satisfied incantation if it is a major payment, as a humorous quip if the amount is trivial (in the latter case the payee will say 'I couldn't sleep at night'). Prices are debated and queried ('How much did they rush you for that?'), and bargaining remains a feature of business in East End markets and shops.

There are several well-established pleasantries for use in shops. Someone making a very small purchase often says 'It's a shipping order' as a humorous apology for spending so little; the shopkeeper also may say it, less amiably, if the customer takes a long time over a ha'porth or is obviously being niggardly. The mention of fourpence never fails to produce comments because this is the legendary 'dirty price'; what a cheap prostitute is supposed to charge. 'That's broke the ice' is a stallholder's saying when he has made his opening sale of the day, and it is said also by a gambler who gets an early winner (compare with the drinking man's cry of 'First today!').

'A couple of bob' is anything but a specific sum. It comes nearest to being an exact amount when a stallholder says 'A couple of bob to you' in answer to 'How much is that, mate?' Otherwise it is best translated as 'some money'. 'Got a couple of bob to spare?', 'I bet that suit cost a couple of bob', 'drop the bloke a couple of bob', etc., are broad statements of principle in which two shillings, or ten pence, is not under consideration at all. One other traders' saying that has passed into wider use is 'shut the shop and bugger the customers': to hell with things, let's put our responsibilities aside for once.

A special feature of small shops used to be the printed notice which said 'Please Do Not Ask for Credit as a Refusal Often Offends'. In its presence, the regular customers habitually had their goods 'on the book' until pay-day. No doubt in many cases it showed the shopkeeper's intention which had proved unrealizable; it served mainly to deter people who were not sufficiently well known from trying for tick. Through continually seeing them, the words were fixed like a proverb (and like the notice in public lavatories for men: 'Please Adjust Your Dress Before Leaving') in every Cockney's mind. A few years ago I saw a parody of them in a cafe a long way from London: 'Please do not ask for credit as a punch in the mouth often offends.'

~ ~

Part of the core of Cockney culture is due to the rural communities from which past generations of East Londoners came. As they flocked in to the riverside areas in the 18th and 19th centuries they reproduced their social customs and close-knittedness in more crowded surroundings. 'Our' street or immediate neighbourhood has the characteristics of a village, the small shop acting as a community centre and information bureau. A number of Cockney practices and sayings have country origins — for example nicknaming: old people in East Anglian villages recall the time when everybody round them had a nickname, and in East London (with more varied material to hand) the habit has persisted.

The view of persons is essentially a rural one. In cities generally, individuals are placed and described by their functions: what they are rather than who. Cockneys are, to a remarkable degree, unconverted to this urban psychology. Their first and continuing interest is in personality and relationships. A typical urban answer to 'Who is John Brown?' might be 'An office worker, has a semi-detached house and a Cortina'; the Cockney type of answer is 'A gloomy fellow, always thinks he's ill, used to go out with a girl from Stepney Green before he married X's sister-in-law'.

Thus, a lot of Cockney description and imagery is personal. Appearance, demeanour, mood, behaviour are all commented on in terms which would be considered intimate or insulting elsewhere. A stylishly dressed individual is a 'flash Harry', a gaudy one is 'lairy'. The latter was 'leary' two hundred years ago. It is used for either sex, sometimes as a type-description as 'one of the lairy-boys' or 'one of the lairy-girls'. To be lairy means, besides showy clothes, strong perfume, rings and bad taste. An item of dress can be deprecated on this account: 'You don't want to wear that, it's too lairy.'

On the other hand, anyone who does not keep appearances up to the social norm is freely criticized. He or she is 'a schlock', 'a slommock' or 'slommocky'; 'scruffy' and 'a scruff' (i.e. a self-neglectful person) were adopted in the 'thirties. 'All anyhow' and 'all over the place' means untidy. A person in a draggle-tailed state is said to look 'as if he's been dragged through a hedge backwards'; if a female is disarrayed, the remark is 'You look like the girl who took the wrong turning' (from the title of a melodrama).

Dirtiness is a disgrace to Cockneys, most of all to women: if their men and children are not as pristine as circumstances allow it is a reflection on them. Their homes too, of course — the highest praise for a housewife is 'You could eat your dinner off the floor in her place'. Of a grubby-looking person: 'he could do with a wash', 'soap and water don't cost much', 'black as Newgate's knocker' or 'black as a sweep'. Nor are these comments made behind their subjects' backs. I have seen a girl in a factory find a note on her machine, from her workmates telling her to wash her neck. Washing is invoked to remedy other failings: the effer-and-blinder advised to wash out his mouth, 'wash your ears out' to one who has not heard something. A perfunctory or inadequate wash is 'a lick and a promise' or 'a cat's lick'; cupping water in the hands instead of using a flannel is 'a soldier's wash'. A wash is also called 'a sluice', and 'a sluice down' means a head-to-foot wash.

Where behaviour is concerned, probably the most condemnatory word is 'monkey'. Used scathingly by itself — 'the monkey!' — it implies a mixture of ignorance and wickedness. 'You bloody monkey!' is for a man guilty of a pernicious act which he will not easily be forgiven. 'Monkey tricks' and to 'monkey about' have the same flavour; they mean mischief in the serious sense, or a performance to which the speaker is hostile and contemptuous. The mildest use is 'little monkey' for a child, but even here it is usually for exceptional naughtiness. 'I don't give a monkey's' is an extreme form of 'I don't care' (imagination can supply the left-off final word).

Cheekiness or back-answering is 'old buck', and this also means self-confident assertiveness. It was a soldiers' word, from Hindu: characteristic Cockney usages are 'Don't give me any of your old buck' and 'He's full of old buck'. 'Carney' is about a different kind of behaviour. It means cunning, but not in the subtle snake-in-the-grass way: 'a carney sod' is a coarse and untrustworthy fellow.

To speak loudly in anger is to 'rort'. The origin of the word is unknown: a Romany connection, perhaps. It is not 'rort off' or 'at', but is complete in itself with or without an object: 'He didn't half rort when they told him', or 'he rorted me all right'. To explode with annoyance is to 'go up in the air' or 'raise the roof', and to enlarge on one's displeasure is to 'lead off' or 'carry on'. Since 1945 'do one's nut' has been widely used, apparently a working-class version of 'blow one's top'.

Somewhere between these is the cryptic 'create', as in 'she doesn't half create'. Create what? Probably a commotion, a scene, or just an atmosphere of vengeance. It implies a lengthy, discomfiting diatribe which is more or less unanswerable. There is also 'palaver', which was brought home by soldiers from Africa in the late 19th century and originally meant a parley with natives. It became the term for confused talk, and then a general to-do: 'a hell of a palaver' means a lot of bother.

Another cut-off phrase in similar vein to 'create' is 'kick up', meaning to protest: 'I'm going to kick up about it.' It is short for 'kick up a shindy' = to make a noisy fuss. Interestingly, the phrase in its entirety is used to give a different meaning: people who are kicking up a shindy are disturbing others' peace, for example by holding a party. The present-day universal semi-polite term for a thorough dressing-down is 'a rollocking'. It may well be, as Partridge thinks, a simple bit of rhyming slang; but it is worth noting that in the 1920s a respectable muscular-Christian story for boys, found on the shelves of public libraries, was called *Jack Rollock's Adventures*. A name so infelicitous virtually asked to be remembered in the language.

On the opposite side of behaviour, a person who fails to kick up when he should and perceptibly suffers from being too reticent is 'backward in coming forward'. He 'lets himself be used as a doormat', 'lets himself get trodden on' (or 'shit on') and 'won't stick up for himself'. If he is very reserved: 'he's so quiet you don't know he's here.' A way of saying that somebody lacks a physical or temperamental attribute is 'he was behind the door when pushfulness was given out' — or behind the door when good looks, brains etc. were given out.

'Aggro' for aggravation was popularized by the skinhead youths of the 'sixties. As a term for strong provocation and trouble, it brought a surprisingly swift change of meaning. Up to that time, in Cockney usage 'aggravate' had always meant to irritate or rub up the wrong way. It was used of children: 'an aggravating little bugger' was one who tried his mother's temper. Men who teased their wives were 'being aggravating', and the demand for it to stop was 'don't aggravate me'. The sense was petty annoyance: a long way from the aggressive new implication of the word.

Terms for exasperation and annoyance are plentiful enough. He, she or it may 'make you wild', 'give you the needle' or 'get on your wick' (the last is possibly something rude in disguise). 'Gives you the pip' means that one has had enough, and covers various kinds of displeasure. It can be equivalent to the present-day 'I'm choked', i.e. fed up and discouraged; but a person also says 'I got the pip and came home' (from a cinema, for instance), meaning that he was bored. 'It's enough to drive you to drink' and 'enough to give you the screaming abdabs' are mock despair. A favourite saying of women who foresee their husbands in bad humour is 'I'll make a pudding and leave home': flee from the wrath to come — the pudding was the supposed contents of the knotted handkerchief which every tramp seemed to carry.

A person who works hard is always respected. 'He's a grafter' or 'he's a worker' is praise. Other versions are 'he doesn't let the grass grow under his feet' and 'I like a show with a bit of life in it'. Somebody who shows deft skill is 'a dab hand at' whatever it is; though this term is also used ironically for practices which can be done without — 'Oh yes, he's a dab hand at vanishing when he's wanted'. Anyone who fails to pull his weight 'dodges the column' or 'swings the lead'. 'Skiving' has been in general circulation since the 1939-45 war and has now produced a meaningful Cockney rhyming expression for the same thing: 'ducking and diving'. An unauthorized rest is 'having a mike' or 'miking'. Stock remarks about reluctance to work are 'born tired', 'he's not afraid of work, he could lie down and sleep beside it', and 'he likes work like the devil likes holy water'.

However, this respect for work does not coincide with the bosses' and managers' keenness to see it done. A zealous foreman is not praised; instead, he 'runs about like a blue-arsed fly'. If he is specially sharp for efficiency, he is 'hot' or 'shit-hot', and those who look like responding to him are told: 'There'll be plenty of work when you're dead', or 'Work will still be here when you're not'. There are hackneyed mock-lamentations of the need to work — 'Roll on, Friday' and (said first thing on Monday morning) 'It's a long week, isn't it?' But a person who in seriousness wishes it were the end of the week, or even home-time, will be told censoriously: 'Stop wishing your life away.'

~ ~

'Gertcher' or 'gertcha', the classic exclamation of Cockneys in books, plays and films (in the 'thirties it was the name of a carthorse in a comic strip), has received a new lease of life from a popular song. It appears in a TV advertisement for beer: cloth-capped men in a pre-war pub growl 'gertcha!' as the song's refrain.

It is authentic; Cockneys have said it throughout this century. Of course the establishment of it as a symbolic word alters the level of its use. Some people still say it and mean it; but increasingly it becomes a 'fun' word. The same thing happened with 'Gorblimey', which used to be taken as a representative Cockney expression. On one hand it was a sure laughter-raiser in a theatre or cinema; on the other, anyone who spoke crudely was described as a 'Gorblimey bloke'. In the end the word cannot be used unself-consciously.

'Gertcha' is 'Get out [of it], you!' contracted. The intermediate stage is 'Gerroutcha'. It does not mean 'go away' in the physical sense. Rather, it is a harsher 'go on!'; it stands for 'don't waste my time, I'm warning you'. However, it can be and often is good-humoured, perhaps accompanied by a playful shove or a pretended turning-away. 'Garn!' is 'go on!', i.e. 'I don't believe you' or 'what do you take me for?'

The other term in this vein is 'shut up!' or 'shurrup!' The nearest equivalent to it is 'lay off': cease. It may refer to talking, in which case it means not 'silence!' but 'nonsense!' Children shout it meaning 'stop' — give over pushing me or following me about; this can be stated explicitly, as in 'shut up copying from my book'. The demand to stop speaking is clear and definite: 'shut your gob!'

CHAPTER 9

Talking Proper

Attempts to represent Cockney speech in print are usually lamentable. The fact that they are made so persistently denotes contempt or condescension; there is a great difference between noting how a person talks and emphasizing the errors (sic) of his every utterance. In most cases it is done carelessly, without due observation, in the frame of mind that correctness does not matter here. Often it is a kind of shorthand using familiar supposed characteristics of Cockney as symbols, like the actors' 'Mummerset' which is 'near enough' for any number of country accents.

One of the few writers who have got near the sound of Cockney was Bernard Shaw, in *Pygmalion*. He did not have the facility his Professor Higgins claimed of being able to place Londoners 'within two miles . . . sometimes within two streets'; Eliza Doolittle and her father are 'cockneys' connected indefinitely with districts round central London. Nevertheless, Shaw took in the vowel sounds which are the deepest-rooted feature of Cockney speech, and his use of them is what makes Eliza credible. The other thing he noted was the Cockney range of tones, the way voices rise and fall when they are being eloquent. Alfred Doolittle's speeches are built on this characteristic.

East London speech is produced chiefly by the throat and lips. Habitually, the tongue is used as little as possible. Thus, the sounds which suffer most are those which depend on firm manoeuvres of the tongue. 'Th' is an outstanding example. When teachers stick their tongues between their teeth to show the correct enunciation of 'through', 'thick', 'bath', 'thought', 'thumb', the children laugh; they have never seen it done before, and the result sounds alien. The hard 'th' in those words is replaced by f, and the softer one — as in 'brother', 'whether', 'baths', 'heathen', etc. — is pronounced as v. When the latter is at the beginning of a word the v sound is less definite and may get near to d; 'they' is not quite 'vey' and not 'dey', but somewhere between the two.

The glottal stop is a direct result of non-use of the tongue. The t in 'butter', 'bottle', 'hot', 'fighting', 'written' and so on can be enunciated only by putting the tongue against the top teeth and moving the lower jaw slightly. Cockneys do not do this; instead, they cut off the preceding vowel sharply. If there is another vowel to follow, as in 'butter' and 'fighting', the break makes a definite throat-sound, and this is heard also when the t ends a word. The most accurate way of writing it would probably be with a symbol for an unspecified incident: 'bi!er', 'ro!en', 'fa!'

In words like 'didn't' and 'haven't' the t is skipped. They are pronounced 'didn' and 'havn'; 'ain't it grand' is 'ainit grand'. Generally, the only exceptions to this are when the speaker is uttering the words slowly for emphasis, and before 'you' and 'your'. In the latter case the t and y are run together to make a sound which is almost ch — 'donchou take any notice'; 'it isnchour turn'; 'ainchou bleedin' ignorant!' As 'ainit grand' indicates, if a vowel follows 'didn', 'havn' etc. they flow into each other to produce glorious combinations: 'carnelpit' for 'can't help it', 'havnarscher' for 'haven't asked you', and innumerable others.

There is no alternative to sounding t when it starts a word. Cockneys then say it clearly, though the tongue is not pushed against the teeth to make a precise middle-class consonant; it touches between the teeth and the roof of the mouth to give something less sharp. The same thing happens, even more loosely, in the compromise sound made when Cockneys want to avoid the crude glottal stop but are still unwilling to be heard talking posh. The tongue moves vaguely upwards; the result is 'gedd-oud of it', 'you'd bedder not'. Sometimes a t and the glottal stop or this d–ish sound can be heard in one word, as 'ta!a', 'pota!o', etc.

Without the habit of using the tongue, r and l are difficult. In Cockney speech, r is pronounced by turning both lips outwards (if the trilled r is mastered, it is a party trick and not for everyday speech.) As for l, many Cockneys cannot manage it after vowels except with the help of a short 'oo' sound which is not made with the lips but breathed inside the mouth. In this way words like 'full' and 'wool' come easily; the others are changed to 'bi-ool' [bill], 'ta-ool' [tale], 'fi-oold' [field] and so on. At the beginning of the last war Jack Warner impersonated a Cockney soldier in a weekly radio show called 'Garrison Theatre' and used the l difficulty for comedy lines — 'a real meal', 'feel ill'. As an East Londoner himself he got it exactly right, and Cockneys recognized and enjoyed the gentle humour.

One other sound which causes a problem is a consonant sandwiched between two letters s: 'lists', 'rests', 'asks', 'posts'. The usual way of getting round it is to emphasize each s but waver to indicate something between them, producing 'ress-ss', 'poss-ss'. However, some Cockneys of previous generations pronounced the middle consonant and threw in an extra vowel to make it easier to say: 'postys', 'wristys', etc. was quite common up to the 'fifties, and a small bakery chain named List's in East London was called 'Listy's' by a good many people before the war.

The dropped and adapted sounds have led to Cockney being called a slovenly speech. (To label it thus fits in with the Mrs 'Arris picture of Cockneys. A wit in the London Magazine in 1907 took up Will Thorne saying that no-one would notice him if he walked through Poplar carrying a loaf of bread: of course, said the writer — that was because they loafed all the time in the East End, ha ha!) There may be a much more concrete reason for them. Up to the last couple of generations, poor people lost their teeth early in life and never had false ones. It was an additional reason why individuals of both sexes looked prematurely old. To pronounce consonants adequately, even with hardened gums, is impossible. How does one say 'th', with the tongue between the teeth, when there are no teeth?

An objection may be that this would have applied in other dialects too. Perhaps it did. However, Cockney is unlike others. They are not confined to a social class; there are 'light' and 'broad' ways of speaking them, but they run all through various localities and communities and the 'broad' is not a speech separated and so given a life of its own. The working-class speech habits and idioms of East London were not kinds within Cockney; they created, and were and are still, the Cockney tongue.

~ ~

In standard Cockney speech h is practically always omitted. It has nothing to do with ignorance; the letter is not left out when the words are written, but in speaking it is treated as silent like the k in knees and knight. One Sunday morning some years ago I sat in a bus behind a man who had his little boy of about four on his lap. The child had a picture-alphabet book, and the father was explaining it carefully; when they came to h, the picture was of a hedgehog. The man said: 'That's an edgeog. It's really two words, edge and og. They both start with h.' As that shows, before the silent h 'a' is turned to 'an': 'an orrible sight', 'an elpless old lady', 'an ot stove', 'an andkerchief', and in every other instance.

The g in -ing endings is also omitted: eatin, drinkin, givin, takin, readin, etc. This does not apply to one-syllable words such as 'wring' and 'thing', so verb forms come out as 'singin' and 'flingin'. There are extra variations in certain -ing words. 'Farthing', 'bleeding' (as a swear-word) and 'pudding' have the end reduced to the minimum: they are pronounced 'fardn', 'bleedn' and 'puddn'. In the past 'anything', 'nothing' and 'something' had k added. Today this is thought uneducated, but 'anythink', 'nothink' and 'somethink' can still be heard. (Another old-fashioned addition is g to make onions 'ungyons'.)

The other dropped letter is d in 'and' and 'old'. 'An' is said in almost every case; as well as 'you an me', it is 'An I'll tell you another thing'. 'Old' becomes 'ol' in front of a consonant, as in 'the ol man', 'silly ol bugger', 'Ol Ford'. When it precedes a vowel the d is usually retained for an easier-flowing sound: 'old Harry', 'my old aunt'.

The indefinite article 'a' or 'an' is pronounced as a short 'er', 'ern': 'er good time', 'wear ern overcoat'. 'An' as abbreviated 'and' is said in the same way. 'The' is pronounced 'ther' — 'ther shop on ther corner' — except when this would cause an awkward collision with another vowel. In that case, 'the' rhymes with 'see' and is run into the other sound in a manner which almost introduces y: 'theeyend of the road', 'theeyartful dodger'. 'To' and 'for' are pronounced 'ter' and 'fer': 'give it ter me', 'go ter bed', or 'fer goodness' sake', 'let's go fer a walk'.

'You' also is 'yer' in the majority of, but not all, instances. If it would sound crude, 'you' is said: it is always 'you and me', and 'thankyer' is rare. 'Yer can't take it with yer', 'told yer so', 'I don't believe yer' are typical usages. 'Your' is always 'yer' — 'take yer coat off'; but 'yours' is pronounced roundly as 'yores'. 'Yer' is 'yes', too, but 'yes' can be 'yerss', 'yep' or 'yeah' as well ('yus' is obsolete except for purposes of amusement).

An 'oh' sound at the end of a word is also converted to 'er'. 'Potato', 'tomato', 'pillow', 'follow', 'tomorrow' are all spoken thus. It offers opportunities to link with the next word in a euphonious wave: 'pillerslip' and 'winderpane' are virtually words in their own right, and after the last war 'barrerboy' came just as naturally. The Narrow Way, the main shopping street in Hackney, is known to everyone as 'the Narraway'.

Cockneys love to make words run together in this way. A lot of exclamations have remained popular for generations because they take the form of a phrase said as one word. Usually they are uttered as feigned surprise or mock indignation — 'Gawdelpus', 'luvaduck', 'corstoneacrow' ('stone a crow', in case it looks difficult), 'GorblindolReilly', 'whatapalaver'. Probably other expressions continue to be used for the same reason. 'Arfapint' and 'twopenny-halfpenny' (pronounced 'tupnyapny', with the middle y launching the second part of the word) are both archaic but enjoyable to say, as are 'upsydaisy' and the alliterative 'black as Newgate's knocker'.

Slurring words and dropping letters serves this purpose to a large extent. When 'of' is reduced to o', pronounced 'er', it can be joined to a word either side. 'Lot of' is 'lotta'; 'end of' is 'enda'; a bottla beer, the toppa the street, a loada crap, tonsa money. One or two of these compounds have found their way into wider use — 'kinda' is well known, and 'pinta' has been picked up for advertizing milk. As the Cockney uses them, they give a different rhythm to phrases. Try 'Hamlet Princa Denmark', or 'in daysa vold', or 'a slicer cake'. In the days of home-made ice-cream children would ask street sellers for 'a taster', which was short for 'a taste of it'.

The same happens with 'to': it is joined to a verb to make a single word such as 'hafta' [have to], 'yewsta' [used to] and so on. In several cases this has acquired its own meaning: 'I've gotta' = I must, 'I'm gointa' = I intend to, or I will. A children's joke of many years' standing is to ask 'Can you do Gazinta sums?' — the answer is 'Two gazinta four, three gazinta six' etc. Partridge has this word in his dictionary as 'guzinters' for entrails and derives it from 'guts and innards'; but it is a variation of the play on 'goes into'.

'To' is seldom used in connection with places. Perhaps Cockneys feel that a journey, however short, deserves to be noted with a more descriptive word. It is 'up' or 'down' a road (correspondingly, either end of the road is the top or the bottom; they are interchangeable). A person on a visit goes 'up his grandmother's', 'round his mate's', 'over Shepherd's Bush', 'down the old man's'. Similarly, route directions rarely state 'go to'; one has to 'cut across', 'nip round' and 'shoot up' various ways. In the days when tallymen tried to catch up with in-accessible or absconding customers, if they asked questions in the neighbourhood the standard answer was: 'There's a pump up Aldgate, mate — go and pump that!'

~ ~

Certain vowel sounds take specific local forms. Cockneys pronounce 'gone', 'off', 'cough' and 'trough' as 'gorn', 'orf', 'corf', 'trorf'. In the past 'au' was pronounced 'ar' in many words (e.g. 'the ratcatcher's darter'). This is now regarded an old bit of illiteracy, but some people still say 'larndry', 'marnder' and 'jarndice'. The 'ew' sound is 'oo' in several words: 'noos', the same 'Soosan', 'stoo', 'nood', 'jooce'. It is 'ew' in others such as 'music' and 'few', and 'oo' is slowly dying out. Another Cockney characteristic is 'agen' and 'agenst' for 'again' and 'against'. Two or three generations ago 'agin' (for both 'again' and 'against') was common, but it is now practically obsolete.

'Et' is East London for 'ate'. 'He didn't oughter et it' was one of Jack Warner's 1940 catchphrases, but it was a little too close to parody; few Cockneys would have stretched 'oughter' to mean 'ought to have'. The rest, with two or three glottal stops, was both correct and amusing. A few pronunciations are survivals of pre-Industrial-Revolution London speech: 'cimetery', 'whilks', 'clerk', 'Derby', 'Berkeley' — the last three being said as they are spelt. Occasionally older Cockneys can be heard using (perhaps only to show that they know it) the 19th-century 'uss' for 'house' when attached to another word: 'workuss', 'washuss', 'shituss'.

However, vowels in everday speech apart from dialect versions have a sound which is uniquely Cockney. They are different from South London and outer-London vowels, and remain a give-away when individuals have 'improved' their speech in other respects. In *Pygmalion* Shaw rendered two of them as 'Ahyee, Be-yee, Ce-yee, De-yee'. In 'Bernard Shaw's Phonetics', by Joseph Saxe, is another attempt based on schoolchildren Shaw heard: 'I, Ber-ee, Ser-ee'. The first of these two is the better. All Cockney vowels are open, but 'a' is never 'i'; it would give 'lite' for 'late', 'pint' for 'paint', 'clime' for 'claim', etc., which are nothing like it.

The 'a' sound is made well back in the throat, with — as Shaw perceived when he wrote *Pygmalion* — a hint of a glide into 'ay-ee'. In the 'father' pronunciation it is well rounded, as if it were followed by r: 'farver', 'barf', 'carm' [calm]. The short a, as in 'fat', is prolonged in contrast with the clipped sound favoured in middle-class speech. It is as if the vowel revives when it is half-way to the second consonant: 'ca-at', 'ma-am', 'ha-and', 'ca-arry'. In practice the change of sound is slight, but sufficient to produce a distinctive vowel.

That is also the case with 'ee', which Shaw has almost right in both his versions. Taking words like 'feet' and 'heap', the opening consonant seems to be pronounced on its own as when children enunciate letters of the alphabet — 'fer', 'her' — and then the vowel picks up in time to meet the end of the word. Short e, as in 'bed' and 'send', is the same as in non-Cockney 'standard English' except when it begins words. Then, it is lengthened at every opportunity. 'En' as a prefix is usually pronounced 'in': 'ingage', 'injoy', 'inlighten', 'inlarge'. A number of the 'ex-' words also are said in that way: 'ixact', 'ixpire', 'ixciting'. In other cases the short e tends towards 'ee', as 'eefect', 'eelectric', 'eescape', 'eestate agent', 'eeconomy'.

R ending a word has a special effect on e (and all the other vowels). The reason is the Cockney's weakness in pronouncing r. Accustomed to producing it solely with his lips instead of using his tongue, he needs another consonant to help form it. 'Brush', 'across', 'trick', 'increase' etc. come out easily; but in words like 'here', 'there' and 'wear' a sound approaching or implying r must be used. The result is 'heeyer', 'theyer', 'weyer'. The y is heard in all words where a, e or i leads to r: chair, fire, cheer, bear, liar and so on. As a sidelight, when some types of working-class dwellings had a space called an 'area', the word was commonly said as 'airy' in East London. This arose directly from pronouncing 'air' as 'ayer'; though the second y was legitimate, the first was necessary, and together they made a mild tongue-twister.

It is a mistake to think, as Shaw apparently did, that Cockneys are oblivious to their own speech-habits. A popular song of about thirty years ago, 'I don't want to set the world on fire', became a special favourite for community singing in pubs and is still in the repertoire because it displays the vowel sound described above. 'I don't want to set the world on FI-YER!' is sung with enormous gusto and amusement. The two notes for the one word allow Cockneys to smile at themselves, and simultaneously to make a collective nose-thumbing gesture at those who would have them speak differently.

~ ~

The Cockney long i is unwriteable. It is open and comes from the throat, as against the genteel 'ai' which is flattened between the roof of the mouth and the tongue. The usual rendering of it is 'oi', but that is thoroughly misleading: 'buy' is nothing like 'boy'. Probably the nearest which can be achieved is a lightly uttered 'ah' changing to 'ee'. On these lines, 'buy' emerges as 'bah-ee', 'like' is 'lah-eek', 'bright' is 'brah-eet', and 'aye, aye' is 'ah-ee, ah-ee'. The exaggerated 'fire' is 'fah-eeyer', the y in all such words a servant of the final r: 'desah-eeyer', 'hah-eeyer', 'lah-eeyer' [desire, higher, liar], and so on.

Short i has one unorthodox use. It is used for the ee in 'been' — 'Where's he bin?' 'It's bin a long time' — and there is a tendency to it in a few other 'ee' words. 'Feel' is often indistinguishable from 'fill', and this is also the case with 'meel'; mealtimes are 'milltimes'. Presumably it is a survival from an ancient pronunciation seen in the general 'tit' for teat and 'britches' for breeches.

The long o is pronounced 'ow' by itself, not 'oh'; the lips round it off and make an 'oo' at the end, and this is the formation of the o in words like 'hope' and 'coat'. When there is a final r to be dealt with — shore, door — the sound is short o (as in hot) with w introduced for the r to hang on: 'sho-wer', 'do-wer', 'o-wer'. It can be heard most clearly when Cockneys shout 'more!' for 'encore!' the vowel has two distinct notes, 'mo-wer!' 'Sure', 'poor' and 'moor' are pronounced as if they were spelt -ore. So are words ending in aw: jaw, paw, claw etc. are said as 'jore', 'pore', 'clore'. When they are used as verbs, r is introduced: 'he stands jawring for hours'.

'Ou' with an r ending also needs a w. 'Our', 'flour', 'hour' and 'sour' are spoken to rhyme with 'tower' and 'flower'. But the short ou of 'out' and 'about' is the chronically misrepresented Cockney vowel. For a hundred years there has been a convention of writing it as 'ah'. Shaw put 'baw ya flahr orf a pore gel' into Eliza Doolittle's mouth: 'rahnd the ahses' is the classic way of conveying East London speech.

It is painfully wide of the mark. Whatever a Cockney's 'out' may be thought to sound like, it is not 'art' — which is what 'aht' would make it. The sound is a lengthened short u. It might be written 'uht', the u as in 'cut' but stretched out; more precisely, it is 'uh-ert'. The phonetic version of a Cockney's 'buy a flower off a poor girl' would be 'bah-eeya fluh-er orf a pore gel'. The 'ya' shows the end of 'buy' used to run on to the next word. Practically any Cockney does this when he talks, but in a street vendor's chant it would become a flourish and almost musical.

'Oo' replaces 'ew' in several instances; in certain words the habit is to pronounce 'oo' like 'ew'. 'Shoes' is usually said in this way, as 'shee-oos'. It may be psychological, due to the feeling that shoes are more refined than boots and should sound so. However, 'you' also gets that pronunciation. 'Ew' made of 'ee-oo' is a really elegant sound, and Cockneys often say 'bee-ootiful' expressively because there is pleasure in enunciating it. 'Tune' does not sound so good; t followed by 'ew' needs careful diction, and is usually exchanged for 'toon' or 'choon'.

U as a letter of the alphabet is 'yoo', and is pronounced thus when it starts a word. 'Usual' is 'yoosual'; 'yooniform', 'yoorine' ('urinal' is 'yoorinal', with a long i), 'yoose' [use], 'yooniverse', 'yoonanimous' etc. follow the same rule. Over words beginning hu- there are different practices. The h is dropped, of course. Technically this leaves things as if it had not been there at all, and a number of Cockneys say 'yooman' and 'yoomorous'. Others treat it as a different case: some say 'ewman', i.e. as they would pronounce it if they did not drop the h, and others fall back on 'ooman' and 'oomorous'.

~ ~

Cockneys have a collection of speech mannerisms and idioms, most of which are 'bad grammar'. The most famous is 'ain't', which was once an upper-class as well as a lower-class colloquialism — it can be found in *Tom Brown's Schooldays*, which describes public-school life in the first half of the 19th century — and almost certainly has been execrated because Cockneys were the people who kept it alive. It stands for am, is or are not, has or have not. In everyday speech it is pronounced 'en' or 'ent' as often as 'aint'. 'It's cold, ennit?'; 'I ent got any'; 'en he stupid!'

'Ain't' is always said fully when it is part of a double negative used in fun. 'Ain't you got no sense', 'that ain't nothing to do with it', 'ain't never had none', and similar phrases employing 'don't', are thrown about mostly for exhibition and amusement and relatively little from ignorance; they are part of the vocabulary which Cockneys enjoy flashing among themselves. That is not to pretend that double negatives are not often used otherwise. They are a means of emphasizing something. 'I haven't had nothing to do with it' is a strengthened denial; a father or mother impressing a warning on a child may say 'Don't you go nowhere near there!' After generations of schoolteachers have condemned the double negative and explained its fallacy, most East Enders know all about it; but they are not disposed to throw away a traditional and useful way of colouring speech.

Another persistent habit is using the present tense for describing incidents: 'There she is, standing shouting at the top of her voice, and her old man's waving his hat in the air, and I'm half-way up the ladder!' It does not happen when facts are being related but is saved for livelier personal details, so a narrator often switches from past to present tense in mid-story. Thus: 'We went down the club last night. It was a bit foggy, so we didn't leave it late coming home. We've just got outside when a fellow walks up to us and says . . .' It is for telling jokes: 'Things are very bad with Cohen, so he goes round to try and tap Rubin for a loan.' What is it but a device for extra animation, to make the story immediate and lifelike?

Tenses are mixed also in 'give' and 'come'. With both words the present is used for the past: 'I give him a piece of my mind', 'She come to see me last night'. There is no explanation of these except custom — a person writing a letter is likely to check with people round him that he should put 'came' and 'gave'. 'Come' has a curious usage in a few sayings, e.g. 'come the old soldier' whch means to try to impose on somebody. There are also 'come the acid' = to be overbearing, throw one's weight about, and 'come the ugly' = to utter threats. A familiar cry of mothers to children is 'Don't come it!', meaning 'don't try those tactics, I know them of old'; an adult version is 'coming it a bit', for an insincere attempt to win sympathy.

The -ly ending to adverbs is frequently dropped: 'he jumped up sudden', 'it's raining steady', 'go careful'. This is not an error but an idiom. When the word has to be emphasized, all Cockneys say it in full with the 'ly' stressed: 'Careful-*lee*!'; 'shut the door quiet*ly*!'; 'eat it slow*ly*!' The syllable is left off for a better sound, or because the adverb in that form is part of an established phrase. 'Piss off quick!' is an admonition meaning 'make yourself scarce'; for urgency, the three words must all be single syllables. (The same is true of 'go slow', of course.)

Up to recent years 'ly' was often replaced by 'like', as in 'he spoke polite-like', 'I acted cautious-like'. This was playing with the syllable and extending it for more effect. Between the wars it was common, until eventually 'like' became a meaningless decoration on any word or phrase. It is not popular today, except for parody, but originally it was an interesting variation in Cockney speech.

'My' is commonly pronounced 'me': 'on me way home', 'breaking me neck', 'I said to meself'. However, it is said 'my' for emphasis, and also when it has any consequence as a possessive pronoun. A person would say 'I'm going down me mother's', but 'My mother is eighty-four'. A long-standing practice is 'us' for 'me'. The children's 'gissit' is 'give us it'; there are 'tell us', 'don't muck us about', 'show us', etc. Its use has diminished in the last forty years, but it remains as a respectable colloquialism.

The grammatical error to which Cockneys are most addicted is 'don't' for 'doesn't' and singular verbs for plural ones. 'He don't care', 'it don't make sense' etc. are regular features of East End speech. Likewise 'things is bad', and 'we/they/you was'; when a story is told in the present tense, 'I goes' and 'they goes' are often heard. Genuine ignorance and imitation of parents account for some of this, but often it is part of a performance. 'I goes and sits down quiet-like' is a talker who likes to entertain.

That is the key to the matter. Speech is an enjoyment to Cockneys, and many 'wrong' constructions are pleasurable to say, or are parts of phrases which would not seem the same without them. 'He doesn't know' is uninteresting compared with 'he donno', when each o is rounded to rhyme with 'dough'. 'We done a bunk' loses most of its vitality if it is changed to 'did a bunk'; 'where was you?' and 'him and me's mates' can be savoured as they are said. Those who disagree, or think the pleasure an immoral one, will be gratified to know that it is slowly dying out through the influence of education. Before 1939 'I were[n't]' and 'he were[n't]' could be heard; they are extinct now, and the other perversions of tense and number are gradually disappearing from the language.

~ ~

'Go' is used to enlarge any verb. The simplest form is 'go and get', 'go and see', etc. However, a Cockney will say 'I've gone and caught a cold', 'he's gone and said the wrong thing'; or 'don't you go and tell anyone'. It means to take a certain step and implies deliberation or being at fault. The full range of tenses is used: 'What do you think she's been and done', 'went and got the sack', 'I'm not going and spending money on that'. But the celebrated 'Now you've been and gorn and done it!' is a Cockney joke. It was devised to fit a musical phrase (children call 'Here we are, we ain't a-playing!' to the same notes), and is spoken for amusement only.

'Go and' is often shortened to 'go' plus a participle: 'don't go moving my things', 'he'll soon go asking for a rise'. With a notable consciousness of tenses, 'gone' and not 'been' is used for the past in this sense: 'I shouldn't have gone telling him', 'have you gone upsetting her?' 'Get' is used when a continuing practice rather than a single action is talked about — 'I get messing about in the garden', 'he got drinking with a crowd', 'you mustn't get worrying over it'.

New usages and vogues arise, of course. The most conspicuous addition to Cockney speech (though it is not confined to it) in recent years has been repeating 'wasn't I', 'didn't he' etc. after sentences. 'Someone gave my car a bang today, didn't they!'; 'he only went and told everybody, didn't he!' ('only' is another present-day term, ironical for some breathtaking act). The idea is to make the sentences more riveting, but they usually fade away because people become sick of them. The 'didn't I!' mannerism was used in the cinema version of *Till Death Us Do Part*, set in Wapping before and during the war; in fact it did not get into circulation until the 1960s.

How much a person uses these sentence-structures and pronunciations is an indicator of 'class', standards of respectability within the working class. It is tempting to think of speech dominated by them and packed with slang as 'typical Cockney', but to East Enders themselves that is low-class. The typical is speech with a good vocabulary in which Cockney pronunciations and expressions are used as natural aids to flow and flavour. Having alternatives available is the key. 'Ain't got none' is a black mark when the speaker plainly knows nothing else. If he says 'haven't got any', the other is at his disposal when occasions permit or make it appropriate.

In most families the children are to some extent discouraged from the 'worst' Cockney speech-forms. They learn them from other children, and the way they talk then depends on different groups' standards. However, it remains a matter of degrees within a framework. When a person is criticized for uncouth speech, the comment is usually on the lines of 'None of us talk like lords and ladies, but that's just ignorant'. Likewise, a mother who is anxious for her children to speak nicely knows the boundaries and will say 'We are working-class but that's no reason why you can't talk decently'. The result is awareness of a choice of language; basically it is always Cockney, but with a meaningful scale of intensity.

Miscellaneous other items: The l in words such as 'walk', 'calm', 'half', 'salmon' etc. is simply passed over, and they are pronounced 'wawk', 'tawk', 'carm', 'arf', 'armshouses', 'sammon'. The hard k or c is not pronounced as Higgins taught Eliza to do it — 'Put your tongue forward until it squeezes against the top of your lower teeth' — but out of the throat; hence, it is often allied with a glottal stop. The 'orf', 'gorn' and 'corf' pronunciation has been used also for 'across', 'loss', 'hospital' and 'foster', but this is disappearing fast: as is 'acrost' for 'across'. 'Yourn' is still used for 'yours', but 'ourn' and 'theirn' are rarely heard now. They have a respectable etymology as contractions of 'your one', 'our one' and 'their one'; if 'mine' is all right, what can be wrong with them?

'Right', an essential word, is a curious survival. It is used as adjective and adverb: 'a right villain', 'a right mix-up', 'right fed-up', 'hurt right bad'. The Oxford Dictionary describes 'right' with this sense as *archaic*. It was used liberally in Jeffery Farnol's historical novels as a characteristic of 18th-century speech, and one of the few accepted uses of it is in Parliament: 'the Right Honourable member', etc. Nevertheless, it has been widespread among Cockneys throughout this century and is a prominent part of their vocabulary today. 'I'm right knackered' is the spot-on phrase for 'I am exhausted', and anyone who gets 'a right mouthful' has been truly told off.

A special East London pronunciation is turning 'gate' to 'git' in the many place-names where it occurs. Aldgate, Bishopsgate, Southgate, Margate are Aldgit, Bishopsgit, Southgit, Margit; Ramsgit, Billingsgit and Ludgit Hill too. Newgate is 'Noogit', Harrowgate is 'Arragit'. This does not apply to the word by itself, so one would say 'a gate in Moorgit'. It is a dialect pronunciation, probably a coarsening of the rural 'get'; and it often stays in the speech of persons who have shed other Cockney characteristics.

~ ~

One of the most striking features of Cockney speech, to many outsiders, is its up-and-down sound. It has been described as 'sing-song', which is apt enough when the speaker has a bad voice; but it can be wonderfully expressive. The East Londoner likes his utterances to be attention-catching whether they are plaintive, indignant, gloomy or humorous. Possibly the idea is caught in infancy, because talking to babies is almost an art-form — a dulcet wheedling down a range of tones. Nagging, anecdote, giving opinions and even greeting a friend in the street are done with the same mobility of voice, to squeeze the utmost meaning out of them, and it is noticeable in ordinary conversation.

By contrast, Welsh and Scots speech are 'musical' through their vowel sounds and the repetition of a characteristic pattern; the west-country rustic has its rolling burr. Locality is not the factor here, however. The Cockney puts strong stress on verbs and adjectives, often exaggerating them to convey feeling. 'You ought to have *seen* it, it was *ever* so *good*'; 'Hall*o*, how *are* you? I was just *talk*ing about you' — the words or syllables lifted and stretched. Nouns are punched out, or said carefully, so there is no doubt what is being talked about; the other words in a sentence may be slurred or run together, as if they are minor accessories to those which give meaning and mood.

It belongs to social class: more specifically, to the Cockney's attitude to emotions. Compare this speech, rising and falling to express sentiments of every kind, with middle- and upper-class speech in which restraint of tone is essential. The content of Cockney talk is unemotional, but the form is all expression. Great importance is attached to the tone of voice, and it communicates how a person feels when the words at face value say nothing of the kind. Almost the opposite is true of socially superior talk — this involves its own subtleties of class distinction, of course. The Cockney's range of expression helps to keep emotions in their place in a way of life which in the past has been unable to afford them.

In manner Cockneys are uninhibited. They laugh uproariously at their own and others' jokes (the middle-class way is to be cool and slightly deprecating when telling jokes: appreciation of one is signified by a smile and a nod). A complaint or displeasure is voiced with all the passion that can be mustered. 'Don't you stand for it!' or 'You tell 'em!' is everyone's recommendation: it means not so much that a case should be stated as that a powerful show of indignation should be made. In each circumstance there is a sense of giving a performance, and those who are the audience know what they expect to see and hear. A colourful remonstration is admired — 'He told him, didn't he!' — and a 'good old moan' has its theatrical element.

Gestures are used a good deal. Some of them are as well-established as stock phrases; they illustrate talk, or can be enacted silently to say much. The wink has a wide variety of meanings. Accompanied by a wag of the head, it signifies happy agreement and approbation: 'That's the stuff!' Delivered straight-faced while someone else is talking, it says 'Don't believe a word he is saying'. It can be for recognition, encouragement or reassurance. When a forefinger is laid beside the nose as the wink is delivered, it means 'Everything is OK, but don't tell anyone what we are doing.'

A suggestion to have a cup of tea is made by moving the forefinger and thumb as if they were tipping the cup to drink from it. Lightly scratching the palm of one hand with the forefinger of the other means that money is required; for example, a delicate way of enquiring about payment for a project might be to say 'What about the — ?' followed by this gesture. To pretend to spit on the palms and rub them together is to express a vigorous appetite for something (it mimes a navvy preparing to grasp his sledgehammer).

There is the 'drop' gesture, and moving the hands beside the ears which is a humorous reference to Jews (they are supposed to do that when they talk). Turning over one's coat lapel as if revealing a badge hidden behind it means the police; a person might do this in a pub or cafe as a hint that plain-clothes police are present, but he would also do it when mentioning them in a story he was telling. To turn the fist upwards and push it backwards and forwards two or three times stands for sexual intercourse (women do this with the arm pointing upwards).

Apart from this sign-language which is familiar to every Cockney, the hands and shoulders and facial expressions all come into play in his speech. To say they are aids to it would imply some difficulty in communicating, and Cockneys seldom suffer from that. Rather, the gestures show how he is animated by the talk. The rise and fall of the voice, the emphasizing of words and making groups of them run together, the pleasures of aptness and imagery, are a verbal culture at work; and not only the mind but the whole person takes part in presenting it.

CHAPTER 10

Make Yourself at Home

Home is the centre of Cockney life. It is where East London boys and girls learn the shades and flavours of their language, the strength of relationships, the attitudes and framework of conduct that are almost ineradicable. Home remains with them all their lives, and attachments to the family are firm.

The terms used for the parts of older types of houses are still used in newer ones, or in figures of speech which no longer apply. 'Home' itself has three meanings. It is, of course, the dwelling and the domestic circle; but it is also the furniture, household articles and knick-knacks. All of these are treated as belonging to the mother — she uses and takes care of them, and they are bought for her. A girl acquiring things in readiness for marriage is 'getting her home together', i.e. the collection of items with which she will make her husband and children comfortable.

Women of an older generation often said, characteristically, 'All my home is what I had when I was first married': they looked after it. A remark still made if anyone knocks over a chair or bumps into a piece of furniture is 'Breaking up the happy home!' (This contains a reference to a short play called 'Humanity', performed in variety theatres at the turn of the century, in which a quarrel between two well-to-do men led to the smashing-up of all the furniture and fittings of a house; working-class audiences watched it incredulously, and it is still talked about at second hand — 'my old man reckons he saw it on the stage years ago'.)

The area outside the front door is still known to everyone as 'the doorstep', even though it may in fact be the landing in a block of flats. Persons waiting or talking there are 'standing on the doorstep', and this occurs in various metaphors. 'On my doorstep' means placed in front of me, for problems, responsibilities and so on; to 'shit on [one's] doorstep' is to court trouble. In these and similar sayings the reference is to more than just the entrance to the home. The cleanliness of the doorstep was, and where applicable is still, an important mark of respectability. A woman's first morning job after the husband and children went out was to scrub the step and whiten the sides of it (this also opened the daily intercourse with the neighbours).

The door itself was always furnished with a black iron knocker, and even today a caller is said to be knocking although he is ringing a bell; and a person who goes on ringing when there is no answer is 'taking it out on the knocker'. Between the wars a man could make a living of sorts by going round with a can of black paint and a brush refreshng knockers at twopence or threepence each. Another front-door tag is for a man using a key at night-time, if he has company of either sex: 'Can't find the hole.' It may sound merely the repetition of a stale joke, but for Cockneys such sayings have a ritual character. If he does not say this, someone else will say it for him; it is an opportunity to invoke familiar realms of awkward sexuality.

~ ~

Hospitableness is second nature, as they say, to Cockneys. An old song expresses it:

> Put your feet on the mantelshelf,
> Go to the cupboard and help yourself,
> I don't care — if your friends have left you all alone,
> Rich or poor, knock at the door
> And make youself at home.

That is the spirit of it (though 'rich or poor' is undoubtedly the sort of thing nobody expects to have to put to the test). In practice, there are well-recognized rules of behaviour. Visitors are indeed welcomed and treated with warmth, but they are expected to conduct themselves decently; one who put his feet on the mantelpiece would quickly be persona non grata.

A visitor, however familiar and frequent, has to knock and wait to be asked in. The only exception might be a specially trusted neighbour who has, perhaps, gained this status by helping in times of illness. A friend who let himself in by the string in the letter-box, or through the back entrance if there was one, would be regarded as taking 'a dead' (= absolute) 'liberty'. 'Liberty' means a grave offence to Cockneys; 'a liberty-taker', one who habitually walks over other people's rights, is a bad character. Another term used in similar connections is 'impunity'. It is said majestically, usually to denote high indignation: 'he walks in and out *with impunity*' means 'he seems to think he can do as he likes'.

There are also degrees in being asked in. Up to 1939 it was quite common for friendly callers to be kept outside on the doorstep and even talk there for long periods. There was nothing invidious about this; often it allowed two people to speak more freely than if they were inside. The wartime blackout more or less ended it. However, it is still normal to keep collectors and officials on the doorstep, and if callers of this kind have to be asked to step inside it is only as far as the passage.

What do visitors come for? To talk — the Cockney's supreme enjoyment. For a number of social reasons visiting has fallen off in the last twenty-five years, but in the past no-one wondered what you had come for. Conversation, gossip, argument were ends in themselves; and, against pressures, this is still the case to a surprising extent. The visitor, asked into the living room, remains mindful of his manners. He does not take a seat until asked; the usual form is 'Sit down, you make the place look untidy', or (probably from the lady of the house) 'Stand up and grow good, eh?'

Hospitality means a cup of tea. A welcome caller, one who will be asked indoors straight away, is greeted with 'If I'd known you were coming I'd have put the kettle on'. If the kettle is already on (a likelihood), it is 'You must have known I'd just . . .'; or 'You must have smelt the teapot'. When people pay a visit away from their neighbourhood and class and find themselves displeased, their condemnation of the alien scene is summarized in: 'Never even got a bloody cup of tea.'

It would be possible to discourse on the East London cup of tea as lengthily and glowingly as Charles Lamb did on roast pig. Orwell thought the secret of its appeal for the poor was its warm comforting quality. Undoubtedly it is addictive; those who are accustomed to it have a craving, expressed as 'I'm gasping' or 'I'm bone dry'. But the chief part of the appeal is probably the social qualities of a cup of tea. As a hospitable offering it is easily superior to the middle-class 'a drink' (alcoholic): the housewife has to go to personal trouble to produce it and see that it is up to standard. Because it is hot, it lends itself to a sit-down and a chat, which are readily prolonged because only the churlish do not have a second cup in the pot. Cobbett, in his *Cottage Economy* in 1822, attacked tea-drinking on precisely those grounds.

The visitor usually announces his departure with 'I'll have to love and leave you'. This may appear to be a misrendering of 'love them and leave them', the behaviour of a ladies' man (or his female counterpart), but it is a different saying. It signifies an affectionate parting, and that the visitor will soon be back. When he or she has gone, the talk may be remarked upon in such terms as 'He's a proper old jaw-me-dead, isn't he?' or 'goes all round the houses when he tells you anything'. But it is not disagreeable: the conversation and the talkers' characteristics have been an enjoyment.

~ ~

The greatest change in the pattern of working-class family life, probably for at least a hundred years, has been brought about by heating. This has affected social life in turn; it makes the transmission of Cockney speech and attitudes from one generation to another far less certain.

Up to about 1950, and previously as far back as anyone could remember, the only warm room was the living room (which until the early 'thirties was called the kitchen, and what is now the kitchen was 'the scullery'). It had either an open fireplace or a cooking-range, and all the activity of the house took place within reach of this. Lighting the fire was the first job every day, and rent-books had a seldom-heeded clause forbidding tenants to chop wood on the concrete of the back yard.

The other downstairs room, known prosaically as 'the front room' ('parlour' is a more genteel word, little used in East London), would have a fire lighted only on special occasions — at Christmas, or for a party; and 'freezing' was taken for granted as the natural wintertime condition of bedrooms. Providing warmth in them was out of the question financially; electric fires were almost unknown in working-class homes, and even the cost of lighting an additional room was regarded as ruinous.

Thus, for most of the year indoors there was nowhere else to be: the living room alone was habitable, except for sleeping. In its small space every evening meals were eaten, children did homework or pursued their hobbies, visitors talked, daughters sat with their boy-friends and sons with their mates, and all listened to the radio; the mother might be ironing at the same time. The conversation was communal, and privacy not expected.

The Cockney's vocabulary and speech-habits have always been formed in these circumstances, surrounded by talk and being impressed with the idea of the glory of phraseology. A non-talker is not a favourite in the home, though 'always got his head stuck in a book' is a partial excuse. When a person does not respond promptly to what is said to him or her, there are trenchant comments to hand. 'No answer, was the stern reply' is one; another is 'Answers come out next week' (a reference to a magazine called *Answers*). The stock of words, sayings and constructions absorbed in this way is almost beyond cataloguing. A great many of them are about nothing in particular but are used simply to decorate or fill out utterances; others are concise and apt.

'Cracked in the right place': a person supposedly stupid who nevertheless looks after his own interests adroitly. 'Toffee': superficial talk or blandishments (the sweet stuff poured over a sour apple). 'And the rest' is a response to an understatement, whether naive or intended to deceive: 'It only costs a few quid' — 'And the rest!' 'A flanker', as in 'he did me a flanker there': a fast one (obviously an old soldiers' term, a manoeuvre against the flanks of an army). A blunder is 'a ricket' — the etymology is unknown, but the construction is always 'made a ricket'.

'Tumble' is to acquire insight into something or somebody: 'I've tumbled you' = 'I know your motives'; 'I've tumbled how the thing works'. It can also mean to find out — 'he got tumbled' — and in that case is available as a noun: 'They used to slip away without paying, but it came to a tumble eventually.' The Cockney version of 'all over the place' is 'all over the shop' or 'all over the auction'. It is used both in a serious geographical sense and figuratively to mean a state of confusion: 'he travels all over the shop', and 'throwing things about all over the auction'. Some expressions live on from the age of horses. A 'gee-up' is a hollow inducement; 'whoa' or 'whoa back' means cool down, go steady; likewise 'in the cart' for in trouble, 'trot' for move briskly (diarrhoea is known as 'the trots'), 'mare' for a difficult-tempered female.

There are the elaborate ironies in which Cockneys delight. 'I'm glad you said it's not raining much', 'glad you told me you'd be here at eight', etc., when the statements have obviously not matched reality. 'I can see that coming off': hopes or intentions not likely to be fulfilled, in the speaker's opinion. 'Pull the other leg, it's got bells on' is an expression of disbelief. 'Getting generous in his [your, her etc.] old age': a meagre contribution from someone who can afford more. 'Fair' means pretty good, but is also used heavily or plaintively to mean its opposite: 'Ain't it fair, eh?' is the classic rendering of 'What have I done to deserve this injustice?' Similarly, 'lively' is for disappointing persons and places: 'you're a lively fellow, you are', 'that pub's lively, I must say'. A stronger verson as regards places is 'a dead-and-alive hole', obviously a corruption of 'more dead than alive'.

The decorative sayings are best explained as that the Cockney would rather say something than nothing. They are sociable, to show a good humour and promote responses from other people, and general accompaniments to whatever is in hand. 'Every little helps, as the girl said when she piddled in the sea'; 'do as the girl says, chance it'; 'let's shut the door and keep the flies out'. Another mildly risqué tag is 'She's a nice girl, but she picks it'. This is used chiefly by girls to cap a conversation about one who is not present. What she picks is a mystery, but the saying is not quite meaningless; it may serve as a warning that the gossip has gone far enough.

'Come round the half-crown side' is an invitation to move to a more convenient spot for seeing or talking — it is an intentional over-statement, and probably means only shifting a chair. 'Little things please little minds' is a comment, usually gratuitous, made when somebody is engaged in a triviality (though it may also refer to idle-minded nosiness). This is gentle twitting, but 'pleased with his little self' is less amiable; it is about smugness, and the 'little' implies contempt. Yet another tag-line is 'lovely, tell your mum' to express satisfaction or thanks. Like other phrases, it is pleasant when kept fresh. Occasionally one finds a man who makes some such remark a habit repeated many times a day, and that is awful.

Exaggeration is a feature of Cockney speech, and the practice of it is quickly picked up by children. It does not mislead anybody; its function is simply to colour-up everything said. 'Big' is always developed into 'whacking great' or 'bloody great', 'bad' is 'diabolical', any degree of intensity is 'something terrible', 'something shocking', etc. A period of time, if more than a few minutes, is 'hours'; or, if beyond the recent past, 'donkey's years ago'. The same dramatization takes place when a person is overdue from an errand or has been longer than briefly in the lav: 'Where you been — China?' The term for ructions or problems is 'murders': 'there'll be bloody murders at work tomorrow', 'it's murders with the old man these days'.

All of this is language used regularly at the present time, generations having learned it from one another principally in the forum of the living room. Today the gathering is dispersed. Young children as well as older sons and daughters use their own rooms and have their friends in them; because of heating, they are separated from the talk and imagery on which their own Cockney is founded. Of course other social changes come into this: the improvement in living standards that has made heating a house instead of a single room possible, the development of education and its effects on the status and consciousness of young people. Nevertheless, it now happens that one calls on an old friend and spends the evening with him in a room alone. His children are upstairs, his wife in another room. The effects on the handing-down of the Cockney language may be profound.

~ ~

Part of the image of Cockneys is quarrelsomeness. They are always ready to take offence; the males throw curses and blows without compunction, the women 'turn the air blue' with their invective. The picture to a large extent is of the old-fashioned slum where people were 'uncivilized', and therefore might apply to a working-class area in any large city; it is about conditions, not character.

However, combativeness *is* a trait of East London culture. Within the framework of social class and impositions they feel they can do nothing about, Cockneys are highly attached to the idea of personal pride. A slight or a breach of the rules of good behaviour is not allowed to pass. Basically it is defence — the East End child is taught early in life to 'stand up for himself' (or herself), and the practical means of defence is vigorous attack.

Over this, the sex-roles are important. The components of manliness are a strong deep voice, the proven capacity for hard work, and general self-assertion. In the past a lot of Cockney men cultivatd the 'boxer's walk', and it can still be seen today: the head and shoulders are moved from side to side like a boxer slipping the punches, and this produces a gait which looks cocky and has implications. Female voices, too, are firm and militant-sounding. If the woman accepts that her husband is ultimately the boss, she has still to defend her home and children — if necessary, to battle with him for their wellbeing. Before marriage she insists on her rights and the respect due to her, and has been schooled in these matters by older Cockney women: at all times of life, she is to stand no nonsense.

But defence is not the only factor. There is a powerful working-class tradition of settling quarrels by prompt open confrontation. Psychologists have recently discovered (though anyone in East London could have informed them) the contrast between it and the vendetta-making and sustained ill-feeling which are more characteristically middle-class. This in itself makes Cockneys appear aggressive. When they are displeased, or something requires to be explained or remedied, there is no brooding over ways to pay the offender out; the queston is dealt with unequivocally, at once. Doing this usually purges anger. Boys who have had a fight 'make up' as soon as possible afterwards (the 'making-up' ritual is a miniature handshake with the little fingers curled round each other's).

To deal with matters in any other way is contemptible to Cockneys. A person who tells tales to get another in trouble is 'putting the squeak in': the word 'squeak' postulates a miserable unmanly voice. This tradition of confrontation has much to do with the popularity of boxing — it is conflict without trappings, and no ill-feeling afterwards.

Through the eyes of other social groups who do not share the Cockney culture or similar inner-city experience, boxing is undesirable largely because the idea of men hitting each other as a sport is incomprehensible. When schoolteachers tell children 'I won't have differences settled by fighting' they are trying to impose middle-class norms of conduct — and probably deeper-wounding behaviour over differences.

None of the foregoing means that the Cockney's answer to everything is a smack in the eye. Violence for its own sake is not admired. Confrontations are usually verbal: a direct statement on the subject in hand, accompanied by forceful expressions to make the speaker's frame of mind clear. The flow of indictment and riposte is often superb, but it is not meant to be comic: each phrase carries its own warning notes. Sayings which are as insulting as they are obscure can be thrown in, such as 'Bend down and I'll buy you a new hat'; 'shut your mouth and give your arse a chance' is another.

Children have their own vocabulary of them. 'Same to you with knobs on' is provocative, and when 'and brass fittings too' is added the situation is tense indeed. The children's epithet for someone who 'squeaks' is 'tell-tale tit'. Adults as well as children use a gibe for a bad loser or a moaner: 'Cry-baby Arden, cried for a farden.' A frequent response to 'I won't stand for it' is 'Then you'll have to sit down for it'. This may be chaffing to take the heat out of matters, or a further inflammation of them.

The Cockney's bark *is* his bite, for the most part. It is used to show and preserve independence, and also to regulate behaviour. It should always be respected, but never feared; for it is seldom malicious.

~ ~

'I can't take you anywhere' is the comment made, usually in mock indignation, when someone is amusingly outrageous. It is carried over from early upbringing — a mother's serious admonition to the child who causes her embarrassment away from home.

'Manners' are important to Cockneys. The absence of courtesy in a person of any age is put down as a sign of negligent parents: 'Where were you brought up?' or 'Would you do that at home?' An adult may invoke this as a cheerful self-excuse: 'I hate greedy kids' when, say, taking another cake; or 'I hate nosy kids' when asking a personal question. These are humorous asides, but when they — or 'Where's your manners?' — really do refer to children they are dire criticisms. ('Manners' is also said instead of 'excuse me' by a person who belches. 'Pardon' is for 'please repeat what you said'; but note that a deliberate 'I beg your pardon' = 'you had better *not* repeat it'.)

Certain habits supposed to be Cockney prerogatives either belong to a distant past or are myths. Drinking tea out of the saucer, for instance. I have not seen it done for forty years. It was done by men in coffee-shops, to cool extra-hot tea and make it drinkable when they were pushed for time; few men would have done it in their homes. Likewise, putting the feet on the mantelpiece was talked about but rarely if ever seen. It is doubtful if it was possible in most living rooms to reach the mantelpiece from a sitting position: as the shelf above the kitchen range, it was about four feet six high on the wall. (The mantelpiece was invariably used as a display shelf. It would hold the clock, favourite ornaments and vases — which in turn held spills, hatpins, collar studs and bills — and as many photographs of members of the family as there was room for.)

A habit which was tolerated until fairly recent times was spitting in the fire. Spitting was practised by almost all men of mature years. It has, thank goodness, largely died out; up to the last war the iron staircases at Liverpool Street station were sickening, and in crowded streets one's shoes or trousers could be caught by a random spitter. Buses and trains had notices prohibiting it inside them, on pain of a fine. (The result was that men spat down from the tops of buses. As the fines differed, there was a 'pleasantry' that spitting in buses was cheaper than on the railways; and other obvious sayings such as 'Never spit against the wind'.) It was assumed to be a necessity, and on that basis spitting in the fire at home was considered moderately hygienic. This helps to explain the 'father's chair' phenomenon in working-class homes: the chair had to be close to the fireplace, for easy reach.

There are clearly-understood standards of behaviour in and out of doors. Swearing, beyond two or three permitted words, and street language are not normally acceptable in the home. 'Street language' means words and phrases which are deemed by convention to be over the borderline of niceness. 'Khazi' and 'tart' are in this category; so are 'gob' for mouth', and saying 'I'm knackered' (for 'I'm exhausted'). The same applies to impolite terms, even when the subject of them is not present. It is unmannerly to speak about a lady as an 'old girl', and a young person who tried this would be told off; while phrases like 'old cow', 'old bag' and 'old boiler' belong to the street corner.

Conventions such as 'ladies first', taking off caps on entering houses, etc., are still strong among Cockneys. Over-familiarity and failing to take one's proper turn are offensive; helping oneself without being told it is all right to do so may produce a sharp 'Don't ask, will you?' A child or adolescent who says 'Eh?' instead of the obligatory 'pardon' is asking

for, and will get: 'Eh to me? Where's you manners!' Indeed, 'eh?' from
a person of any age is treated as a sign of ignorance, and he or she is
likely to be mimicked critically.

All this reflects community standards and ideas of self-respect. It
does not involve pretence. Home is also the place where each individual
makes himself comfortable. Standards of domestic comfort vary today
as never before, but it always takes precedence over show. The parlour
as the room where the best furniture stood unused except to impress
visitors was a feature of lower-middle-class suburban life, not of East
London. The long-standing rule in receiving visitors is 'take us as you
find us', and it is meant literally. The onus is on the visitors to be
decently dressed and behaved, and this applies to everyone outside his
or her own home and intimate circle — or the verdict will be 'I can't
take you anywhere'. Perhaps this is a suitable point at which to note
that Cockneys are the only people in Greater London who do not call
the theatrical and high-living area 'the West End'. To them it is 'the
Other End': polarity.

Not surprisingly, a certain amount of Cockney metaphor over
behaviour comes from the meal table. Anyone who changes his mind
because it is advantageous to do so 'talks as his belly guides him'. The
proverb 'waste not, want not', whatever the context, is usually capped
with 'pick it up and eat it'. Similarly, any emphasis on the word 'more'
leads to 'Don't have any more, Mrs More' — a music-hall song about
food. The person who surrenders delicacy to practicality by picking up
an awkward piece of food is bound to say 'fingers were made before
forks'.

Another response, by a man to his wife in a not-too-serious exchange
of words, is: 'I don't care what you call me as long as you don't call me
late for my dinner.' A less obvious connection is in 'he [she, I] was
behind the door when looks' — or brains, or cheerfulness, or any other
useful attribute — 'were given out'. It recalls that in crowded
households it was possible to be overlooked, and the treats went to
those who made sure they were noticed.

~ ~

Children are expected to, and do, appreciate their homes and respect
their parents. Father is 'dad' or 'pop', and 'the old man' when speaking
of him outside home, as mum is 'the old lady' (never 'my').
Grandparents are 'grandad' and 'granma', but in talking about them
this name by itself is reserved for the pair who live nearest or are seen
most often; the others are distinguished as 'other granma', 'Poplar
grandad', etc.

'Aunt' and 'uncle' are less precise terms. Besides their correct applications, they may also be used for close friends of the family who are not related at all. A second-cousin is likely to be called 'uncle' or 'aunt'. The idea is for the young always to address the grown-up people in their circle with respect. An outsider must choose titles carefully when he speaks about one member of the family to another; he must never be derogatory, and inappropriate terms can be a slight which will be taken up immediately.

'He' and 'she' in place of names or titles are considered belittling. They might be used at work, for bosses or unpopular colleagues, or in a deliberately contemptuous reference such as 'her across the road'. Within the family they are not tolerated, and their use (negligently, or in a bad temper) will bring a rebuke at once: 'Talk properly, if you please', or 'Who's *she*, the cat's mother?' In the music-hall sketch 'My Pal Jerry', Nobbler said 'Mind who you're calling. There's jerries and jerries, but my Jerry's got a handle on.' It was a chamber-pot joke, of course; but it was based on the well-understood principle of courtesy over names.

Parents' relationships with their children go through stages which clearly reflect economic life. The small child is cosseted and played with. It must have constant attention; modern theories of rearing which say that the child should not be picked up when it cries are regarded as stupid and callous by Cockneys. However, the sex-roles and the need for independence are borne in mind. The child is soon going to be told that it is 'a big boy' or 'a big girl' now; the cosseting dies away sharply — 'getting too old for that sort of thing'.

This is the point at which a barrier begins to grow between children and their fathers. It depends on the family's financial standing; but, given the normal restricting income, they become to some extent an alien force insistently forcing demands on him. What they require is measurable in work time. In the past a man would often say 'I've got to work half-an-hour for that sixpence', and the thought is still present today. It is not until the children have left school and are self-supporting that they can meet their father on good personal terms, without resentment; then, the relationship frequently flowers.

There are other consequences of this economic restraint. A boy or girl who feels that things are wrong in the home — say, in the father's treatment of the mother — has not the right to say anything until he or she is earning and contributing to the household upkeep. In the 'thirties, boys who won scholarships were often spoken of as softies ('pansies' or 'cissies'): not for studiousness, but because it was thought unmanly to go on being a dependent after the age when the majority left school and worked for wages. This view still hangs round remaining at school and going to college. The unvarying Cockney comment on student radicals and youthful intellectuals, 'never done a day's work in their lives', refers to it. The point is not to impute laziness, but that as non-earners they have no standing with the community.

Throughout the children's growing years their mother is the dominant influence, and their behaviour is her concern. A difficult child is 'awkward', 'contrary' (pronounced to rhyme with Mary — 'oh, you contrary little devil'), or 'cussed'. The last, pronounced 'cussid', is a survival from older generations raised in the country. Crying is 'blaring', 'grizzling', or 'turning on the waterworks'. A pushful child (or adult) is 'not backward in coming forward', and a wilful little girl is 'a bit of a madam'. This is also a form of address which has a better-mend-your-ways implication. 'My lady' and 'miss' mean disapproval, and 'I'll *pay* you, madam' is a dire warning.

Even when the husband takes a good share of the household chores, his wife sees them all as her responsibility. Part of the reason is that she knows other people judge her family on that assumption; the social climate has not changed very much in this respect. When the family's demands for her attention and services are too clamorous, she cries sarcastically 'Wait a minute and I'll dance for you for the other ha'penny'; or 'Would you like me to pick you up and sing to you as well?'; or 'What did your last servant die of?' She is rueful over her own foolishness in waiting on them: 'I'm only the onion.' This refers to the flavouring in a stew — its absence would be bemoaned, but its presence and function are taken for granted. It is not so: few sections of society make mothers the objects of so much affection and respect as Cockneys do.

What about the gatherings of the extended family — grandparents, aunts, uncles, cousins and their children — which have always been an important element in East End life? 'Localized kinship' has suffered adversities in the last twenty years, but the kinship impulse is still conspicuous. East Londoners who have moved (or, more to the point, have been moved) regard it as a natural obligation to see the old man and the old lady frequently; married daughters often make considerable journeys for regular visits to their mums. Relatives keep in touch to a remarkable extent, simply because it is unthinkable not to do so.

The street parties for the Jubilee in 1977 provided a telling demonstration of the pull of kinship and neighbourhood. Members of families returned to their parents' streets all over East London, and brought their own children. In the evening they had parties in the houses. It was not just a getting-together; the occasion meant going home, and they had no doubt where it was.

One other figure in many Cockney households is worth mentioning: the lodger. He had no place in family life, and was a shadowy background figure whose comings and goings were nobody's business but his own. His generic nickname is unforgettable, however. He was the Artful Dodger. It was a rhyme, and a joke on all the jokes about the lodger as seducer, and it remains one of the many little gems of inventiveness in the language.

CHAPTER 11

The Future of the Language

The last thirty years have seen few additions to Cockney and many erosions of it. The way the wind is blowing was shown in a mid-day television programme in April 1979. Three young East Londoners played and sang the piece they had written, with 'Gertcha!' as the key-phrase of its refrain. Interviewed afterwards, they said they thought 'Gertcha!' was a term 'worth preserving', and they hoped to do more like it.

Unfortunately, a language cannot be preserved piecemeal in that way. For all its wit and tunefulness, to the degree that the song is popular it will help to extinguish 'Gertcha!' more quickly. The life-spans of catchphrases have diminished as the media have multiplied. A conspicuous difference between the great music-hall performers and present-day ones is that the former introduced little new material. Characteristically, each had a repertoire of a dozen songs with memorable words, and the audiences did not want to hear different ones.

But they were heard perhaps five or six times a year. The advent of recording, then of radio, made repetition more frequent and listening less a matter of specific choice. Songs and phrases were worked until the audiences had too much of them, when they were dropped and fresh ones introduced. The process is so intensified today that a line or mannerism usually passes from the everybody's-lips stage to oblivion in a very short time indeed.

Thus, phrases from music-hall songs have remained as standard Cockney sayings simply because they were never over-'exposed'. 'One of the ruins that Cromwell knocked about a bit', 'don't dilly-dally on the way', 'one of the early birds', 'where did you get that hat?' — it would be possible to list fifty songs from the 1920s and the beginning of the century. Up to 1939 a common East End saying for a ridiculous situation was : 'What's this, Karno's?' It referred to the Fred Karno burlesque comedy show which appeared at music halls before the first world war; the idea of a present-day TV comedian or show being a proverb for forty years is almost inconceivable.

When radio was the supreme family entertainment in the 1930s and 1940s it produced lines to be repeated, but they were much shorter-lived. Arthur Askey's 'Aythangow!', 'what would you do, chums?', 'if ever a man suffered', 'don't be higgerant' — the life-span of these and others was two to five years. Their period of widespread use was followed by an absolute decline, as if people were unconscious of ever having used them. The present-day life-span tends to be shorter still, perhaps two years at the most. (The ITMA phrases — 'can I do you now, sir?', 'after you, Claude', 'don't forget the diver', etc. — were an outstanding exception, chiefly because they were rooted in the wartime period which was itself unforgettable to a generation; but thirty-five years after they originated they are becoming incomprehensible.)

However, there is another important difference. The music-hall phrases were often taken from the streets to be used in songs and comedy. 'Don't dilly-dally', 'any old iron', 'the likes of 'er' and 'Ginger, you're barmy' are examples; the stage rendering did not 'preserve' them, since their existence was not in question, but gave a special flavour and status to them. Other catch-lines such as 'has anybody here seen Kelly?', 'when father papered the parlour', 'a little bit off the top', contained the essence of Cockney everyday speech and badinage. 'Aythangow!' was in the same tradition — it came straight from the bus or tram conductor calling out for fares — but, in the pre-war radio situation, was worked to death.

Without this background of familiar use the phrases do not reflect living language, and to talk of 'preserving' them implies that organic life has already gone. There is much more to Cockney than 'Gertcha' and 'don't dilly-dally', but less than there was and should be if all were well. Has Cockney a future?

~ ~

Since it is a community's language, the answer depends on whether that community and its culture survive. Despite the scholarly tracing of linguistic roots, Cockney as we know it arose in the 19th century. It compounded the older London 'vulgar tongue' with the speech-structures and traditions brought in first by countryside immigrants and then by Irish, Jews and other Europeans.

The strength of these influences can be seen by looking at the census returns for the East End districts in 1851 and 1861. In teeming populations, only a minority among the older generations gave a local birth

place. Large parts of the riverside area were dominated by families
fresh from Ireland. Essex, Suffolk, Kent and Surrey are commonly
recorded, and women often came from places much farther afield —
presumably having come to London as domestic servants.

The influx itself fostered other elements, in particular the costermongers who by the end of the century were thought to symbolize
Cockneydom. To immigrants in all times and places, trading is a vital
source of language. Selling food and household wares to an industrial
population without time or facilities to grow its own produce, the
costers spread their lingo with its cant and Romany borrowings
through the East End. Terms for money, goods and people were
perforce picked up quickly and indiscriminately, and with them came
pronunciations and idioms.

The mixture produced a distinctive language in an astonishingly
short period because of one other factor: overcrowding. When St
Katherine's Dock was built in the late 1820s, 11,300 persons were
made homeless by the demolition of 1,250 houses: an average of 9½ to a
house. Leaving aside the ghetto conditions described by reformers
(Jack London in 1902 cited reports of 25 and even 45 to a house in
Spitalfields and Hoxton), nine or ten people remained the normal
occupation for a house in East London up to 1939. In a medium-length
turning there could be nearly a thousand men, women and children.

Houses were commonly shared, and the layout of 19th-century
streets confirmed the cheek-by-jowl existence. A number of East End
streets were built as 'courts', with no roadway but only a pavement
between the lines of front doors. They were ready-made theatres of
social life, as the music-hall show 'Casey's Court' demonstrated. (The
only surviving court-street is Parfett Street, off Commercial Road.) In
Limehouse several of the side roads were so narrow that the women
hung out their washing across them, using one another's upstairs
windows.

Everything in daily life reflected and extended this continual inter-
mingling. Today one could almost believe that there is an
administrators' conspiracy to prevent people talking to one another.
The outstanding feature, of course, is the replacement of terrace
housing with blocks of flats: no hanging-out washing, garden fences to
talk across, street doorsteps and being participating spectators of the
coming and going of the neighbourhood. The isolation has become an
inducement to vandalism and robbery, leading to protective measures
which are degrees of further isolation.

At the same time, the population of East London is falling. Clearance schemes and lack of work are responsible. An edition of Harold Clunn's *The Face of London* published in the 1960s says, concerning St Katherine's Dock: 'the Port of London Authority have plans for the modernization of these docks, contrary to the report that they are to be dried up and the space devoted to a continuous promenade with parks, restaurants, concert halls, etc.' Since then the docks all down the river have been closed, and St Katherine's has become a marina with a hotel attached (housing promised as part of the scheme has not materialized).

In the 1880s Charles Booth thought the docks had no future, as the age of sail was ending. Had he been right, at that time other industries would have pushed their way into East London. Planning regulations prevent this happening today, with the result that the loss of the docks and everything which stemmed from them — down to lorry-drivers' cafes — is virtually an absolute loss of employment. The residents of Tower Hamlets, the borough which comprises Stepney, Poplar and Bethnal Green, say there is 'no work here': the surest source of decay.

Changes in the hours and organization of shops also contribute to the loss of community. Closing at five-thirty or six has created a minor revolution in social life: the streets are empty in the evenings. Pre-1939 shop hours, anarchic and exploitative as they were, provided large-scale social intercourse of several kinds. It was possible to take a night-time stroll through the market or round the shops expecting to meet persons you knew and to chat with them. Activities which depended on numbers of people in the streets have ceased: such as street-corner political meetings (at which the level of information and argument was considerably higher than it is in television discussions today).

What takes place in shops has altered to the same effect. The old system of serving at a counter meant that standing in a group waiting for one's turn was taken for granted, and they were places to meet and talk. A woman returning from shopping would say that she met this or that person in the grocer's or that she had a conversation with somebody she previously knew only by sight. When another member of the family had been out to a shop he or she was asked 'Was anyone in there?', i.e. whom did you see and what gossip did you hear? The self-service shop does not exist for that sort of thing. To stand about is to be an obstruction; and there is even a half-hostility among the trolley-pushing customers, something like that of motorists each of whom wants the others to get out of his way.

Objectively, the changes have been for the good. No-one would wish back the conditions of the past: crowded housing with primitive amenities, long working hours, streets polluted by horse-dung instead of traffic fumes. Some of the loss of contact is due to higher living standards all round — people do not walk about the streets and parks because they can watch colour television in comfortable living-rooms or go out in cars. Yet it is remarkable that a great many East Enders are conscious of the price paid for improvements, and are thoroughly regretful. This is not the rose-coloured-spectacles view of persons who escaped hard times: it comes from a lot of those who experienced the worst. They say that human warmth and the sense of belonging have gone, and that these made life worth while as material gains do not.

The sociology of all this is far-reaching, but without doubt the Cockney verbal culture has suffered. A language flourishes on spoken use. Indeed, the decline of literacy that is lamented so much nowadays may be directly connected with people's inability to get together and talk. Not long ago I saw some election addresses published by Labour municipal candidates in East London in 1902. They were reasoned arguments on the state of society, with references to history and theories of social evolution. No left-wing party would dare to issue such an address today: all would agree that working-class people could not possibly understand it. Apparently in 1902 they did understand, for the candidates were elected.

One measure of the loss of vitality of Cockney is the absence of nicknames for decimal coins. The new coinage took over in 1971, after a lengthy introductory period in which everyone in Britain was encouraged to 'think decimal'. After several years, not one of them is known by other than its formal name. The terms for the old coinage are still used in sayings with wider meanings — 'tuppence', 'a couple of bob', etc. — but the present-day tokens are 'two pence', 'ten pence', 'fifty p'. It is impossible to imagine this being the case fifty years ago. The seven-sided fifty-pence piece and the microscopic half-penny would have been given titles which in turn would make similes for personal and social comments.

~ ~

In view of these tendencies, the future of the Cockney language seems limited. However, tendencies have a habit of hanging in the air — they remain pressures and discouragements, but do not come to the expected fruition. For a hundred years small one-man and family businesses have been pushed towards extinction, until theoretically they should not exist at all today; yet they continue to proliferate because, against the odds, large numbers of people are attached to the idea of personal independence.

Similarly, Cockney speech is not going to die out. Its special characteristic of being a working-class language ensures that. For the foreseeable future East London will remain predominantly an area of low-grade employment and housing. The authorities appear unwilling to supply amenities for it, and the rest of London regards it as an insalubrious island to be kept away from. If these seem harsh judgements, there is plenty of evidence for them. In the winter of 1976-77 there was a prolonged strike at the Whitechapel sorting office, and mail for the whole of East London was held up for many weeks. At the end of it, a local paper commented bitterly that the strike was hardly mentioned in the national press: had it been anywhere else, frantic protests would have resounded, but this was only the East End. Try living there. You will find that the majority of your friends in other parts of London don't want to come to see you: they think they will fall off the edge of the earth.

In those circumstances there is obviously going to be a population conscious that it is treated as low-down in terms of social class, and it preserves attitudes, speech and a general culture formed by a century and a half of this. The tendencies are simply to devitalize it and arrest further development of the language.

A possible source of new energy for Cockney in the future is the Asian immigrants. At present nearly all of them are first-generation, and they do not mix. Their numbers are not comparable with those of previous waves of immigrants; currently there are probably 20,000-plus Sikhs, Pakistanis and Bengalis in the main East London borough of Tower Hamlets, as against the 40,000 Jews from eastern Europe who settled in Stepney alone between 1881 and 1901.

In the 1960s the Asians were mostly males, but they are now families. Their chief employment is in the garment trade which runs all through the East End and formerly was almost all-Jewish; the economic reasons are the same, and conditions in the workshops (and for home-working) are not very far above those of the sweatshops of fifty years ago. But the Asians' children go to school among the white population. As members of a despised section, they learn the 'worst' English — that is, Cockney; and, in reversal of the usual process, take it home and pass it on to their parents. The outcome may be not only an affirmation of Cockney speech-habits, but an enrichment of the language from Urdu, Tamil, Bengali, etc., as has happened with Romany and Yiddish in the past.

The effects of the media on Cockney should not be judged too quickly. The comic Cockney is still there, of course, and the last twenty years of television, radio and the films have seen the growth of a 'realistic' drama in which Cockneys and other regional types play a large part. Leaving aside questions of trueness to life, this makes amusing or picturesque features of all the dialects available for everyone to pick up. Lots of southerners now say 'chuck' for 'pal' or 'dear', 'yer what?' for 'you don't say so!', 't'ra' for 'cheerio', having learned them from 'Coronation Street', 'Z Cars' and so on. Likewise, many Cockney expressions now have a national currency. From that point of view there is a general fusion of ways of talking; none is private property any more.

It remains to be seen what this will lead to in a longer term in the use of words and idioms. Possibly it has already blighted a good many and, devalued for their original users and adopted only as novelties by others, they are on the road to being discarded. Yet the Cockney tongue contains numerous things which other people have had and cast off, because in the Cockney verbal culture they are highly serviceable. If — and it is undoubtedly a big 'if' — that culture remains strong enough, it may again become the melting-pot for whatever expresses working-class circumstances, moods and standpoints.

~ ~

The factors working for and against the survival of Cockney are social rather than linguistic. Is a future for it desirable? A sentimental answer, in the vein of 'those were the days', does not help at all. It is like wishing back the times when bus fares were a penny and chair-menders came round the streets, overlooking the grinding poverty at the bottom of them.

For whom should it be desirable: for Cockneys themselves, for society as a whole, or both? The only valid criterion is what can be broadly called the health of society. It is healthy to have and be part of a living community, unhealthy when there is only a collection of alienated individuals. It is better to have than not to have dependable relationships. If there are to be restraints on behaviour, it is better for them to come from a general feeling of responsibility than from a legal apparatus.

A lot of time has been spent, too, trying to persuade the working class that they do not exist any more but have been 'embourgeoisified' and risen to the exalted level of 'lower middle class'. Whatever the purpose of this — probably commercial rather than a sinisterly political one — it simply is not true for the large populations of East London and the other inner cities. On the other hand, various left-wing groups do not credit the working class with any intelligence but see them as fodder for being 'radicalized.'

Thus, a sense of identity is needed. This, and the closely-knit culture arising from it, was the foundation of Cockney. It clearly embodies a high degree of social health; indeed, one reason why the Cockney fascinates many people may be that he appears sound and uncomplicated, with all his dreadful ways, in what is widely said to be a sick society. Keeping a language alive does not in itself ensure that state of affairs, of course. The language is the outward sign, the glowing complexion of an individual in rude health; but it also feeds back, creating an atmosphere in which the makings of good health are recognized and prized.

~ ~

It would be cheering to hear protests at times about crude and careless misrepresentations of Cockneys' speech and their way of life as a whole. Comedians and Mrs 'Arris's successors presumably have to be put up with, but there is no reason why anything and everything should be allowed to pass. A short time ago, a radio newsreader announced that taxi-drivers were complaining of night-time 'violence in the East End of London'. She then gave the districts they named: all were in south-west and north-west London. There have been other similar instances. One is left with the impression that practically all rough or nefarious behaviour can be casually attributed to the East End. That is where it all happens: did not Jack the Ripper do his murders there (even though the experts agree that the Ripper himself was not an East Ender — only his victims)?

Again recently, the writer of a gossip page in the *Evening News* offered a prize for the most amusing 'Cockney rhyming slang' his readers could invent. The results were what would be expected: scraps of bright verbiage for reading, not speaking. But why 'Cockney' for this kind of thing? The implication is that any idiotic phrase or epithet can be called 'Cockney' if it is a rhyme.

This might appear a trivial annoyance, but it is not so puny if the name of some other group is substituted. A competition for examples of the way Jews are reputed to speak, or made-up pidgin-English to take the rise out of Asians, would lead to complaints to the Press Council. The Irish have become sensitive to being shown as Pat and Mike who utter howling inanities every time they speak. How are Cockneys supposed to feel? (Curiously enough, in the *Evening News* contest the only semblance of Cockney was when the columnist himself suggested 'Anthony Blunt', after the professor-spy, as a disguised obscenity for an unpleasant fool. Apparently he did not know that Cockneys have had such a term for years — not 'berk', but 'Joe Hunt'.)

As regards radio and television plays, it would achieve a good deal if the drama departments of the BBC and commercial companies sometimes employed an adviser on Cockney speech. Even when the failings are minor, they are conspicuous and often discrediting. A boy shouting 'Give us an 'and': a single syllable makes it all wrong, for it should be 'Give us 'and' said almost as one word. The difference is not just the form but the whole sound, and the boy is suddenly revealed as a youthful actor who has not been coached well enough. The slang expressions and swear-words, often overdone or used inappropriately; sentences phrased as no Cockney would utter them. A certain amount of guidance in these things would not only produce the realism which is sought after, but make Cockneys feel that they were being represented decently instead of imitated without due regard.

In Cockneyland itself there are now a few centres — some of them community organizations, others developments of the libraries — which have drawn in local people to record aspects of their lives and culture. Several small books of reminiscences and photographs have been brought out, and a large amount of material is on tape. History has been the preoccupation, for the understandable reason that people with clear memories of life and work before (and even after) the 1914-18 war are becoming fewer and fewer. However, similar considerations apply in many ways to the Cockney language, and a serious effort should be made to record not only voices but memories of past usages and influences.

There are dangers in this kind of thing. It can become a variety of anthropology, inviting middle-class observers to pore patronizingly over the East End; or produce a self-conscious folksiness. But unless the attempt is made in the near future, some keys to understanding Cockney will be lost. A lot of its etymology is obscure and arguable today because it has not been thought worth bothering about. To a large extent, only Cockneys can explain why Cockneys say the things they do. Many of the scholarly explanations of words, phrases and pronunciation are wrong because they are linguistic ones, when the origins are in happenings and prosaic facts of life.

On the other hand, proper explanations are often bypassed in favour of the myths about Cockney. As an instance, in the last decade the criminals'-slang term 'grass' has come into fairly common use, chiefly through the police dramas on television; in case anyone does not know, it means a police informer or the act of informing against one's associates. An enquiry about its origin was published in a newspaper in 1979, with a reply which said it was rhyming slang (again!): a contraction of 'grasshopper' to rhyme with 'copper'.

This does not even make sense — an informer is not a policeman but a member of the public, usually himself a criminal. A likelier guess at the origin of the word is that it has to do with 'snake in the grass' or a similar expression; it embodies the idea of treachery. There are probably people who can enlighten us about things like this, by recalling that they once existed in a different form which makes the origins clear. The point is not to collect etymologies for scholarship's sake, but to affirm what the nature of Cockney is and stop the knockabout explanations taking over.